WITHDRAWN

D1362254

The Scopes
Trial

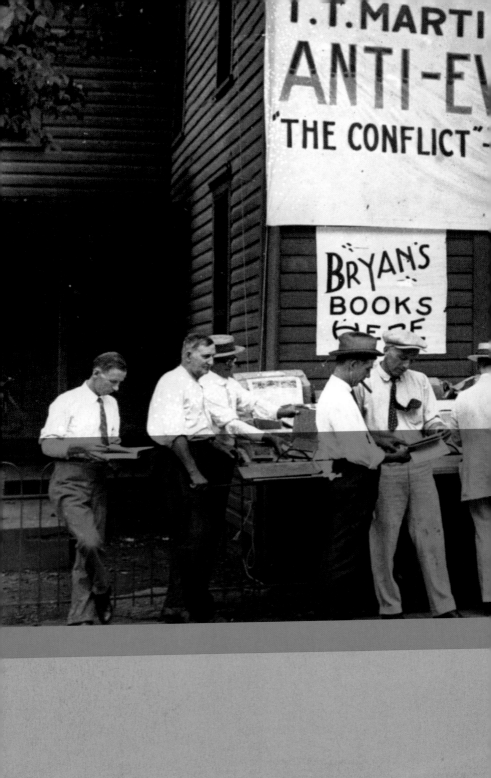

PERSPECTIVES ON

The Scopes Trial

Faith, Science, and American Education

MICHAEL BURGAN

Marshall Cavendish
Benchmark
New York

Copyright ©2011 Marshall Cavendish Corporation

Published by Marshall Cavendish Benchmark
An imprint of Marshall Cavendish Corporation

All rights reserved.

No part of this publication may be reproduced, stored in a retrieval system or transmitted, in any form or by any means, electronic, mechanical, photocopying, recording, or otherwise, without the prior permission of the copyright owner. Request for permission should be addressed to the Publisher, Marshall Cavendish Corporation, 99 White Plains Road, Tarrytown, NY 10591. Tel: (914) 332-8888, fax: (914) 332-1888. Website: www.marshallcavendish.us

This publication represents the opinions and views of the author based on Michael Burgan's personal experience, knowledge, and research. The information in this book serves as a general guide only. The author and publisher have used their best efforts in preparing this book and disclaim liability rising directly and indirectly from the use and application of this book.

Other Marshall Cavendish Offices: Marshall Cavendish International (Asia) Private Limited, 1 New Industrial Road, Singapore 536196 • Marshall Cavendish International (Thailand) Co Ltd. 253 Asoke, 12th Flr, Sukhumvit 21 Road, Klongtoey Nua, Wattana, Bangkok 10110, Thailand • Marshall Cavendish (Malaysia) Sdn Bhd, Times Subang, Lot 46, Subang Hi-Tech Industrial Park, Batu Tiga, 40000 Shah Alam, Selangor Darul Ehsan, Malaysia

Marshall Cavendish is a trademark of Times Publishing Limited

All websites were available and accurate when this book was sent to press.

Library of Congress Cataloging-in-Publication Data

Burgan, Michael.
The Scopes trial : faith, science, and American education / by Michael Burgan. — 1st ed.
p. cm. — (Perspectives on)
Includes bibliographical references and index.
Summary: "Provides comprehensive information on the *Scopes* trial, evolution, fundamentalism, and American education and the differing perspectives accompanying them"—Provided by publisher.
ISBN 978-0-7614-4981-2
1. Scopes, John Thomas—Trials, litigation, etc. 2. Evolution (Biology)—Study and teaching—Law and legislation—Tennessee. 3. Fundamentalism. I. Title.
KF224.S3B87 2010
345.73'0288—dc22
2009035648

Editor: Christine Florie
Publisher: Michelle Bisson
Art Director: Anahid Hamparian
Series Designer: Sonia Chaghatzbanian

Expert Reader: Edward J. Larson, Ph.D., Professor and Hugh & Hazel Darling Chair in Law, Pepperdine University School of Law, Malibu, CA.

Cover: John T. Scopes (left) and attorney Dudley Field Malone (right) listening to jury's verdict.

Photo research by Marybeth Kavanagh

Cover photo by Bettmann/Corbis

The photographs in this book are used by permission and through the courtesy of:
Getty Images: Topical Press Agency, 2–3; Hulton Archive, 22, 45, 66; Chicago History Museum, 29; Time Life Pictures/Mansell, 53; Bridgeman Art Library, 57; Dorling Kindersley, 69; Lara Jo Regan/Liaison, 82; *Corbis*: 16; Bettmann, 8, 31, 40, 47, 72; Underwood & Underwood, 16, 34; Justin Lane/epa, 77; *The Image Works*: Topham, 10; *The Granger Collection*: 51

Printed in Malaysia (T)
1 3 5 6 4 2

Contents

Introduction

AMERICANS VALUE RELIGION AND CHERISH the right to worship as they choose, which leads to a variety of faiths across the country. Throughout the country's history Christianity has been the dominant religion. One type of Protestant Christianity has called for strictly following the rules set down in the Bible. Many of its followers have tried to influence public life, based on their beliefs. Now known as fundamentalism, this strain of Christianity has a long history in America.

The United States has also been greatly influenced by the thinking of the country's eighteenth-century creators of the Constitution. As a group, they championed the power of reason and knowledge to improve life. Although they believed in God, the founders also saw that mixing religious beliefs with public life—particularly promoting one official state religion—could lead to intolerance and division. Their concerns led to the passage of the First Amendment, which allows freedom of worship, but also bars the national government from favoring one religion over another. The amendment also guarantees freedom of speech.

Despite the First Amendment protection of religious worship, many Americans continued to see their country as a

Christian, specifically Protestant, nation. During the 1920s fundamentalists thought new ideas and values threatened Christianity in the United States—and perhaps the country itself. To them, one of the greatest dangers was the theory of Darwinian evolution. This theory implied that God did not create humans; rather, they developed over hundreds of millions of years, tracing their origins to simple organisms. The fundamentalists thought Darwin's theory was wrong and that teaching it could weaken faith in God among Christians.

In July 1925 a Tennessee teacher named John T. Scopes became the focus of a legal battle between those who supported the teaching of evolution in public schools and the fundamentalists who opposed it. The foes of fundamentalism included such people as Clarence Darrow, one of the lawyers who defended Scopes. Darrow was not a Christian, and he thought the fight against evolution reflected the fundamentalists' attempt to promote their religious beliefs over all others.

Darrow was already well known before the *Scopes* trial. So was the leading attorney for the state of Tennessee, William Jennings Bryan. The fame of these two men brought international attention to the trial. So did the clash of ideas between science and religion.

John T. Scopes lost his case, but support for the theory of evolution based on natural selection—what some people call Darwinism—has gained support in the world of science. At the same time, many fundamentalists continue to battle against the teaching of evolution in public schools. Some Americans take a middle ground and believe that people can be Christian and still accept evolution. Still, the conflict between fundamentalists and those who believe in evolution shows no sign of being resolved.

One
The Trial of the Century

THE TOWN OF DAYTON, TENNESSEE, with a population of less than two thousand, had never seen anything like it. Perhaps no small town in America ever had. In the center of Dayton local leaders closed the streets to traffic. Newspaper reporters and camera crews flooded the town's hotels, and Chicago radio station WGN prepared for the country's first live broadcast of a legal trial. Along the town's streets, vendors erected small wooden stands where they could sell hot dogs, lemonade, and souvenirs. Dayton seemed like it was preparing for a circus or a major sporting event. Instead, everyone in town—and even people around the world—was waiting for a criminal trial to begin.

The accused was John T. Scopes, a twenty-four-year-old teacher in Dayton. The young man had recently graduated from the University of Kentucky, then went to Dayton to teach science and help coach the high school football team. Scopes was considered shy but likable, and he had already made a good impression on the residents of Dayton. In the days before the trial he marveled at the attention it had

A large crowd attending the *Scopes* trial gathers outside the Dayton, Tennessee, courthouse.

drawn. He later wrote, "The town was filled with men and women who considered the case a duel to the death."

On one side were devout Christians, often called fundamentalists, who believed in the story of creation described in the book of Genesis. God had created all life on Earth, including humans. Some fundamentalists also asserted that this creation took place in just six twenty-four-hour days,

John T. Scopes was charged with violating Tennessee's Butler Act, which forbid the teaching of evolution in the state's schools.

as the Bible claimed. The fundamentalists had demanded passage of the law that turned Scopes into a criminal. They opposed the teaching of human evolution in public schools.

In January 1925 Tennessee lawmaker John Washington Butler introduced a bill that said any school receiving public money could not teach "any theory that denies the story of the Divine Creation of man as taught in the Bible." Almost a hundred members of the Tennessee General Assembly voted for the bill, which became known as the Butler Act. Just eleven opposed it. Tennessee governor Austin Peay signed the bill into law, though he did not think it would be enforced. He saw the Butler Act as a symbol of the concerns state fundamentalists had about evolution. The governor never could have imagined the national attention the Butler Act would bring to his state.

The Road to the Dayton Courthouse

On the other side of the "duel to the death" was a variety of people who opposed the Tennessee law and supported the teaching of evolution. Some interpreted the Tennessee Constitution as forbidding the use of religion as the basis for laws, which the Butler Act seemed to do. Others asserted that evolution was a fact, and students needed to know the truth about biology.

Butler's law attracted the attention of a New York group, the American Civil Liberties Union (ACLU). It saw the Butler Act as an attack on academic freedom and free speech. Teachers had to be free to explore what was true and to teach ideas that many people might reject. By the 1920s the idea of academic freedom was accepted at many colleges, though not at all schools with ties to churches. And public high school teachers, like Scopes, faced greater pressure to teach

The Fundamentalists

In 1910 a California millionaire named Lyman Stewart began using some of his wealth to publish the writings of religious scholars. The essays were published in a series of twelve books called *The Fundamentals: A Testimony to the Truth*. Stewart and the authors wanted to outline and defend the basic teachings, or fundamentals, of Christianity. In 1920, perhaps reflecting the Stewarts' efforts, the term *fundamentalist* was used for the first time as a name for Christians who supported these basic beliefs. The fundamentalists feared what they saw as the growing influence of atheists, those who reject the existence of God, and agnostics, those who believe people can never know for sure if God exists. Many fundamentalists also believed that every word in the Bible was literally true and came directly from God. The fundamentalists led the attack against the teaching of evolution during the 1920s. Today's fundamentalists continue to battle against evolution being taught in schools.

what was accepted in their communities. Tennessee fundamentalists argued that since their tax dollars supported the schools, they should have a say in what was taught. That thinking helped the supporters of the Butler Act. The ACLU then sparked the *Scopes* trial by offering to provide legal defense to any Tennessee teacher who challenged the law.

In Dayton an engineer named George W. Rappleyea read about the ACLU's offer. A native New Yorker, Rappleyea had moved to Dayton for work. He was a modernist Christian who believed that God and Darwin could exist side by side. He disliked the idea of the state placing limits on the teaching of evolution. Rappleyea went to town officials and suggested Dayton arrest a local teacher for promoting Darwinism so the ACLU would come to town and challenge the Butler Act.

Dayton officials did not feel strongly one way or the other about the Butler Act. But they realized the attention a trial could bring. Dayton had once been a major town in Rhea County, but local businesses began to suffer when a large employer closed. The town saw its population fall by more than one-third. A test case of the Butler Act, they hoped, would bring people into Dayton. The visitors would spend money, and the newspapers' attention would, as one resident said, "put Dayton on the map."

With the town officials and then local attorneys on board, all Rappleyea needed was a teacher to arrest. He and town leaders called John T. Scopes to the drugstore, where they were hatching the plan. Scopes had been filling in for an ailing biology teacher. He told the men that he had been using the standard Tennessee high school textbook for biology. The book did describe Darwin's ideas on natural selection, which left God out of the act of creating life

The ACLU

The American Civil Liberties Union developed in response to the U.S. government's efforts to limit freedom of speech and other rights during World War I. The government saw the restrictions as necessary for winning the war. Defenders of civil liberties saw them as unconstitutional acts. In 1920 the ACLU emerged out of an earlier group formed to protect civil liberties. Its members believed the First Amendment gave Americans the right to speak freely and assemble to discuss any ideas—even the overthrow of the government. The group's creed said, "All thought on matters of public concern should be freely expressed, without interference. Orderly social progress is promoted by unrestricted freedom of opinion."

Opponents of the ACLU pointed out that Roger Baldwin, the group's leader, had gone to jail for refusing to serve in the military. He had worked with groups that opposed the U.S. government and its economic system. A New York State Senate report said the ACLU "is a supporter of all subversive movements. . . . It attempts not only to protect crime but to encourage attacks upon our institutions in every form."

Today, opponents still attack the ACLU for defending the rights of all people, even those accused of carrying out acts of terrorism. The ACLU responds that the Constitution demands equal treatment for everyone, even those who oppose the United States. Protecting free speech in any form is still one of its major concerns.

John Scopes (seated center) and town leaders re-create their meeting at Robinson's Drugstore, where they began to plan for Scopes's arrest.

on Earth. "Then you've been violating the law," the head of the local school board said.

In reality, Scopes had never gotten to the section on evolution, but he opposed the Butler Act and knew the importance of the theory of evolution to modern science. Scopes was not religious, though he did not actively oppose religion. He did think, as he later said, "The Butler Act was an effort on the part of a religious group, the fundamentalists, to impose by law their religious beliefs on the rest of society." Scopes agreed to let himself be arrested so the ACLU could defend him and challenge the Butler Act.

Scopes was arrested on May 7, 1925. Two days later he had his first day in court, with two local attorneys by his side. One of them was John Randolph Neal. The first hearing was to decide if there was enough evidence to try Scopes for breaking the law. Neal told the court that evolution was not in conflict with the Bible. In addition, Neal argued that the state had no right to define scientific or religious teachings and to force them on public school teachers or students. He said it was un-American and unconstitutional "to limit the human mind in its enquiry after truth." Neal and Scopes himself never denied the prosecution's claim that Scopes had violated the Butler Act. (This was despite Scopes's later admission that he actually did not teach Darwinism to his class. He was

John Randolph Neal, one of Scopes's attorneys, speaks before the court regarding evolution, the Bible, and the teaching of both in the classroom.

The Tennessee Textbook

The biology textbook John T. Scopes used in his classroom had been approved by the State of Tennessee before the Butler Act was passed. *A Civic Biology*, by George William Hunter, was written in 1914. In it Hunter mentioned the importance of Charles Darwin's description of evolution and natural selection. Evolutionists since Darwin's time had noted the many similarities between humans and monkeys and apes, and Hunter did as well. (That connection led some people to call the *Scopes* trial the "Monkey Trial.") The author also discussed heredity, the idea that traits are passed from parents to children.

Hunter's book was current for the time and sold well. But his ideas on evolution led him to conclusions that many people would oppose today. Hunter wrote that humans had evolved into five distinct races and that each differed from the others in "instincts, social customs, and, to an extent, in structure." He claimed that "the highest type of all" were the Caucasians, "represented by the civilized white inhabitants of Europe and America." Early Darwinist thinking sometimes led to such racist notions. It also shaped a concept called eugenics, whose followers hoped to promote the higher evolution of humans by weeding out weak members of society. One way to do this, eugenics supporters said, was to prevent the mentally ill, criminals, or other so-called undesirable people from having children. Such a restriction would prevent them from passing along their unwanted traits to children. William Jennings Bryan and other Americans opposed eugenics and saw its rise as another harmful aspect of Darwinism.

supposed to, and he would have, if he had not mistakenly skipped the section.)

Since everyone agreed that Scopes had broken the law, the case moved forward, setting the stage for one of the greatest legal battles in American history. It featured the clash of two powerful ideas: God as the creator of everything versus evolution and the random development of humans and other species. The *Scopes* trial, as it came to be known, also pitted two of the country's best-known lawyers against each other. As the two sides publicly presented their arguments, Scopes himself faded into the background, and the leading lawyers on either side of the duel took center stage.

Two

The Legal Giants

Across the United States William Jennings Bryan was known as the Great Commoner, as he generally supported average, working Americans against the interests of the wealthy and powerful. Trained as a lawyer, Bryan had won his greatest fame in politics. In 1896 Bryan delivered a rousing speech attacking economic policies that favored the rich. That speech, and others after it, marked him as one of the greatest public speakers in U.S. history. Yet despite three tries to win the presidency, he failed each time. Many Americans, however, still considered him an important figure.

Bryan was also a deeply religious man. He read the Bible often and said it guided his life more than any other book. He eagerly returned to practicing law for the first time in almost thirty years so he could join the prosecution in the *Scopes* trial and defend the Butler Act. His presence seemed fitting, since Bryan had worked hard for the passage of the Tennessee law.

Faith and Evolution

At the start of World War I Bryan served as President Woodrow Wilson's secretary of state. Bryan opposed U.S. entry into the war. Fearing Wilson would find a way to

The well-known William Jennings Bryan, a proponent of the Butler Act, defended it in the *Scopes* trial.

send troops to Europe, Bryan cited political differences with Wilson, resigned his office, and began to speak out against the war. Bryan also opposed Darwinian evolution and the theory's effects on America. He particularly disliked an offshoot of Darwin's theory known as social Darwinism, which seemed to suggest that the rich and powerful owed nothing to the poor. Social Darwinism contradicted Bryan's view of Christianity, in which people had a duty to help the less fortunate.

Social Darwinism

Charles Darwin did not like some of the ideas of social scientist Herbert Spencer, but the two men became linked after Darwin began using a phrase Spencer coined: "survival of the fittest." Spencer researched human interactions within society. Like Darwin, Spencer believed that the strongest members of a species survived, thrived, and passed down their traits to their offspring. Unlike Darwin, however, Spencer did not see this as a random process. To Spencer, evolution was moving toward a goal of progress, certainly for humans if not other species.

Spencer's ideas appealed to those who believed in progress and the value of competition. Letting the strongest (or smartest, or hardest-working) people achieve whatever they could in life helped the species as a whole. Governments should not hold back the strong or do much to help the weak. These ideas came to be called Social Darwinism.

After the United States entered the war, Bryan read two books that further shaped his thinking. *Headquarter Nights,* written by the American professor Vernon Kellogg, said that German officers during the war made the link between Darwin's theory and their military efforts. The Germans saw themselves as the strong who were rightfully wiping out the weak. British author Benjamin Kidd argued in *The Science of Power* that Darwin had a direct influence on the thinking of the German philosopher Friedrich Nietzsche. The German thinker denied the existence of God and suggested that "supermen" had a right to rule. Bryan agreed that Nietzsche had been influenced by Darwin, and the German's ideas demonstrated to him how Darwinian thinking could harm society.

Bryan had once accepted the basic idea of evolution, but by 1921 he actively opposed teaching it in public schools. By this time evolution was commonly taught at colleges and public high schools. In high schools the first textbooks to include the theory tended to stress a type of evolution that set aside Darwin's concept of natural selection. By the 1920s, however, new discoveries made Darwin's name more prominent, even while natural selection was still not stressed. And in the field of genetics, more work was being done that lent weight to his theory of natural selection.

In 1921 Bryan gave a speech called "The Menace of Darwinism." The speech was later published and sold well to fundamentalists. Bryan argued that "the natural tendency of Darwinism is to lead those astray who put their faith in evolution." Bryan knew that not all evolutionists were atheists, but he thought those Christians who accepted the theory were even more dangerous to the faith. "While claiming to believe in a Creator, he [the Christian evolutionist] puts God so far away that consciousness of God's presence loses its power to comfort. How can one be conscious of God's presence in his daily life if God has never, since life began, touched a human heart or put His hand upon the destiny of nations or individuals?"

Removing Darwin from the Schools

Bryan did not oppose science or the teaching of facts. But he believed that students should not learn ideas about creation that could not be proven. He called the theory of evolution a "guess." Bryan also said citizens had the right to control what was taught in the public schools they supported through taxes. If fundamentalists thought evolution destroyed religious faith, which in turn harmed society, they had a right to speak up. Bryan said people should not be expected to pay for the teaching of "atheism, agnosticism, Darwinism, or any other hypothesis that links man in blood relationship with the brutes [animals]."

For Bryan the battle against evolution was not just about defending God and the Bible. Bryan had won some political support from Americans who opposed modernism. These people tended to be from the South and West. They lived in small towns, and many were farmers. In the words of historian Richard Hofstadter, they supported a "revolt against modernity"—any changes in society that seemed to threaten their religious views or traditional way of life. Those modern ways were spreading quickly across the country with the rise of motion pictures and the development of radio.

To a degree, some of Bryan's supporters questioned the value of education beyond high school. They saw cities as dangerous places. They feared the call among some

A Minister Takes on Bryan

Bryan's attack on Darwin and evolution brought a quick response from Harry Emerson Fosdick, a Baptist minister. In 1922 Fosdick wrote an article for the *New York Times* that criticized Bryan. Here are some of his views:

> When Darwin . . . ventured his hypothesis in explanation of evolution—a hypothesis which was bound to be corrected and improved—one may say anything else one will about it except to call it a "guess." . . . Today, the evolutionary hypothesis. . . is, as a whole, the most adequate explanation of the facts with the regard to the origin of species that we have yet attained. . . . [E]very fact on which investigation has been able to lay its hands helps to confirm the hypothesis of evolution. . . . [Bryan] proposes to take his science from the Bible. He proposes, certainly, to take no science that is contradicted by the Bible. . . . [T]he Bible is for Mr. Bryan an authoritative textbook in biology."

reformers for government to take a greater role in ending social ills. On the last issue Bryan might have had some disagreement with these Americans. But on the whole he shared their values. He wanted to defend those values and the people who held them. Bryan believed that the elite teaching in universities and working in business opposed those values — and supported the teaching of evolution. Bryan was ready to challenge them.

In 1922 Bryan gave a series of lectures called "In His Image." Bryan believed that, as the Bible said, God had created Adam, the first man, in his image. Bryan's goal, he said, was to confirm "the faith of men and women, especially the young, in a Creator, all-powerful, all-wise, and all-loving, in a Bible, as the very Word of a Living God and in Christ as Son of God and Saviour of the world. . . . My purpose is to prove, not only the fact of God, but the need of God, the fact of the Bible and the need of the Bible, and the fact of Christ and the need of a Saviour."

Bryan's call touched a nerve among fundamentalists. In twenty states voters pressed lawmakers to make it illegal to teach evolution in public schools. Bryan became the national leader of this movement. He said he did not really care if the theory of evolution was correct. Right or wrong, teaching it weakened the Christian faith in the young. It led them to challenge their elders and authority figures. Defenders of evolution said that was the point of education — students learn to challenge accepted beliefs in a quest for the truth. Even so, Bryan and the fundamentalists kept fighting for laws against the teaching of evolution in public schools. They scored their first success in Tennessee with the arrest and trial of John T. Scopes.

Attorney for the Defense

Bryan agreed to join the prosecution against Scopes on May 13. Meanwhile, the ACLU was assembling a legal team to send to Tennessee. ACLU president Roger Baldwin realized the case would put "the Good Book against Darwin . . . or, as popularly put, God against the monkeys." Baldwin wanted to find lawyers who accepted that religion has some role in society yet still supported academic freedom. Others who supported Scopes suggested that Clarence Darrow would be the perfect lawyer for him. Like Bryan, Darrow was famous. Unlike Bryan, he was an agnostic who saw danger in Christian teachings, or at least the ones of fundamentalists. A clash between Bryan and Darrow would draw even more attention to the case.

Darrow, who was from Chicago, had just defended two teens in a case that shocked many Americans. Richard Loeb and Nathan Leopold came from wealthy families, and Loeb had recruited his friend to help commit a so-called perfect crime: the kidnapping and murder of a younger boy. Darrow was appalled by the facts of the case, but he also opposed the death penalty and did not want to see Leopold and Loeb executed for their crimes. And in the U.S. justice system, even a person accused of committing the most hideous crimes has a right to the best legal defense possible. The Leopold and Loeb case was one of many trials in which Darrow defended people most Americans hated or feared. By the time his career ended, Darrow was sometimes called the Attorney for the Damned.

Darrow was eager to join Scopes's defense once he learned that Bryan would be on the prosecution side. "At once I wanted to go [to Tennessee]," he later wrote. "My

Attorney Clarence Darrow looked forward to joining Scopes's defense and publicly challenging William Jennings Bryan's views on fundamentalism.

object, and my only object, was to focus the attention of the country on the programme of Mr. Bryan and the other Fundamentalists in America. I knew that education was in danger from the source that has always hampered it—religious fanaticism." To Darrow, trying to replace scientific evidence with biblical teachings was synonymous with ignorance. Many scientists across the United States agreed, and they supported Darrow's efforts.

A Man of Strong Words

Along with Clarence Darrow and William Jennings Bryan, a third well-known American shared the stage in Dayton. H. L. Mencken was a Baltimore journalist who wrote about a wide variety of issues. He pointed out stupidity and corruption wherever he thought it existed. For the *Scopes* trial Mencken turned his attention to Bryan and the other fundamentalists who attacked evolution. Mencken called Bryan "a poor clod like those around him, deluded by a childish theology, full of almost a pathological hatred of all learning, all human dignity, all beauty, all fine and noble things. . . . He was born with a roaring voice, and it had a trick of inflaming half-wits." Mencken's was an extreme representation of the views of educated Americans who opposed the fundamentalists and their battle against evolution.

The ACLU reluctantly agreed that Darrow could join the defense team, though, as Scopes later wrote, the group feared "the trial would become a circus." The ACLU's greater fear was that Darrow's strong views against religion would hurt Scopes or the ACLU's fight to protect civil liberties in general.

As the ACLU feared, Dayton did indeed become something of a circus as the July trial date neared. People came to Dayton to see Bryan and Darrow or to support their favored cause—religion or evolution. Vendors sold stuffed monkeys and other monkey-related souvenirs, along with food and drinks. One man brought a trained chimpanzee to entertain tourists. The town had one of the largest courthouses in the South, but even then, town leaders feared they would not

A woman stands before the Dayton Courthouse with a monkey doll and a sign reading, "They can't make a Monkey out of Me."

have enough room for the crowds they expected. They built a stage outside, where people could listen to the trial through speakers or gather around to hear broadcasts of the trial.

Some fundamentalists came to Dayton to sell books and to make speeches, while signs hanging from buildings said such things as READ YOUR BIBLE DAILY FOR ONE WEEK. The people of Tennessee, belonging mostly to various Protestant churches, on the whole, were deeply religious. No one could question which side most of the crowd supported as the "trial of the century" prepared to unfold.

Three

The Trial Begins

On July 7, Bryan arrived in Dayton by train. Several hundred people greeted him at the station, and a small parade formed as he rode through town. Darrow arrived two days later but received much less public attention. Finally, on July 10, 1925, the Great Commoner and the Attorney for the Damned entered the Dayton courthouse. Joining them were several other attorneys on each side, Scopes himself, and about a thousand curious watchers. These included a hundred or so journalists who would report on the trial for the world.

The judge for the trial was John Raulston. He, like most of the Tennesseans in the courthouse, was a religious person. He was active in the Methodist church and held generally fundamentalist views, though he said he did not have strong feelings about evolution. Raulston was also eager to get his own share of the national attention that was focused on the case. Darrow later wrote that Raulston never turned down a request from the newspapers to have his picture taken.

First Conflicts

The day was hot, with the temperature hitting the nineties. The mass of bodies crowded into the room only added to the heat.

Police officers on either side of Raulston waved large fans, as they tried to keep the judge cool. For Darrow the weather wasn't the only thing getting him hot. He was angry to see a READ YOUR BIBLE DAILY sign in the courthouse and to hear a minister give an opening prayer. After the first session Darrow and his team told Raulston "that in a case of this nature, especially, we did not consider it fair or suitable to play up their side by opening court proceedings with prayer." The judge refused to stop the opening prayers.

The first business of the court was selecting a jury. All the people in the pool of possible jurors were men. Most were farmers. Some had never heard of evolution; some had, but they did not have a strong opinion about it. One man was a minister who admitted he had preached against evolution.

Each session of the *Scopes* trial began with prayer. Though the defense team objected, Judge Raulston overruled it.

He was not selected. Of the twelve jurors finally picked, eleven of them were members of Christian churches. They heard only some of the courtroom debates, however. During the first few days of the trial, Judge Raulston often asked them to leave when the lawyers were discussing certain legal issues. He would decide the issues and then present his decisions to the jurors.

The lawyers' opening statements were delivered on Monday, the thirteenth. For the defense, John Randolph Neal stated that the charges should be dropped. He said that among other reasons, the Butler Act violated the Tennessee constitution. Like the U.S. Constitution, Tennessee's document guarantees freedom of speech and religion. Arthur Garfield Hays, another defense lawyer, compared the issue to the Roman Catholic Church's efforts to deny the scientific ideas of Galileo Galilei and Nicolaus Copernicus hundreds of years earlier. The church had refused to accept scientific facts that disputed its teachings about the nature of the universe.

Tom Stewart, a state attorney, presented the main thrust of the state's case against Scopes. The Butler Act, he said, was "an effort on the part of the Legislature to control the public school system, which they have a right to do." The state wanted to keep the case focused on this narrow issue, rather than on religious beliefs or academic freedom.

Darrow, however, said that of course the case was about religion. The Butler Act stated that teachers could only use the "divine account" of creation found in the Bible as an explanation for the appearance of life on Earth. By calling that account divine, Tennessee was putting the Bible above all other religious or moral writings. The law, Darrow said, "makes the Bible the yardstick to measure every man's

An Early Conflict between Religion and Science

For centuries the Roman Catholic Church accepted some of the scientific ideas of the ancient Greek thinker Aristotle. The church argued that Earth was at the center of the universe, and all other bodies in space revolved around it. This notion matched the Catholic belief that humans were God's most important creation, and so their home was at the center of everything. During the sixteenth century Nicolaus Copernicus discovered that Earth and the other planets orbit the Sun. During the seventeenth century Italian scientist Galileo Galilei came to the conclusion that Copernicus was right and publicly defended his theory of the solar system. Catholic officials threatened Galileo with torture if he did not deny that Earth orbits the Sun. Galileo agreed, though in private he still supported Copernicus. During and after the *Scopes* trial defenders of evolution sometimes referred to Galileo and his famous struggle to assert scientific views that opposed religious teachings.

intellect, to measure every man's intelligence, to measure every man's learning."

Some newspapers praised Darrow's speech. The *Chicago Tribune*, one of Darrow's hometown papers, called it his greatest speech ever. The *New York Times* reported that "the Tennesseans who crowded the room leaned forward in tense attitudes of attention" as Darrow's "words fell with crushing force." But despite the strong defense arguments, the charges against Scopes remained, and the trial continued.

The Fight over Experts

Several days later the defense battled with Judge Raulston on another issue. The lawyers wanted to call scientific and religious experts to the stand to discuss the evidence for evolution and to show that some Christians believe in it. They also wanted this testimony to be in the court record. The defense hoped to use it to their advantage when they appealed the case. In fact, the ACLU expected to lose in Dayton all along. It wanted the case brought to federal courts, where the defense thought it had a better chance of winning.

The legal debate over allowing the experts to testify sparked some of the first heated exchanges among the lawyers at the *Scopes* trial. Hays told Judge Raulston, "The eyes of the country, in fact of the world, are upon you here." Prosecuting attorney Herbert Hicks replied, "This is a court of law, it is not a court of instruction for the mass of humanity at large." Hicks and the other prosecutors did not want to argue the scientific truth of evolution versus the biblical creation story.

As the two sides argued, prosecutor Ben McKenzie asked Hays, "Do you believe the story of divine creation?" Hays did not, but he quickly replied, "That is none of your business." The prosecutors wanted the jurors and the people following the trial to see that Darrow and his team were agnostics, if not worse. The defense, however, had tried to show earlier that they were not out to attack all religious belief. Dudley Field Malone, a Roman Catholic, said for the team, "While the defense thinks there is a conflict between evolution and the Old Testament, we believe there is no conflict between evolution and Christianity."

Bryan Speaks

During the debate over allowing the experts to testify, Bryan gave his only speech as a lawyer for the state. He began addressing the issue of expert testimony, but then he moved on to the way evolution denied the role of God in creating humans. Bryan asserted that no one had ever found proof that one species evolved from another. "And yet they call us ignoramuses and bigots, because we do not throw away our Bible and accept it as proved, he said." Bryan would not throw away his Bible, and he refused to believe that God was not at the center of all creation.

Bryan also suggested that Clarence Darrow believed that teachers and what they taught could harm young students. Specifically, in the Leopold and Loeb murder trial, Darrow said one of the young men had been influenced to kill by what he read in school—the works of Friedrich Nietzsche. Darrow denied he had tried to say teachers who assigned Nietzsche were responsible for the Leopold and Loeb murder. To prove Darrow was wrong, Bryan read Darrow's words from the court record of that trial.

Bryan spoke for a little more than an hour, and the crowd listened closely to every word. Scopes later wrote that he

The Search for "Missing Links"

In the years before the *Scopes* trial Darwinists often talked about "missing links"—animals or early humans that directly connected modern humans to their ape ancestors. After Darwin's death scientists found some fossils that did provide clues of human evolution. Another one seemed to turn up in 1912. Found in Piltdown, England, the pieces of bone were said to be part of a skull that had both human- and apelike qualities. The so-called Piltdown Man turned out to be a fake; someone had combined an orangutan jaw, some chimp's teeth, and a human skull to create the "fossil." Despite that fraud, other fossils discovered since have shown the evolution of humans over millions of years. Some scientists still talk about "missing links" that fill the gaps between one stage of evolution and another.

was "not listening to what he was saying, but to how he was saying it. . . . The longer he talked . . . the more complete was the control he had over the crowd."

Dudley Field Malone, not Darrow, rose next to speak. Not known as a great public speaker, Malone dazzled the courtroom with his challenge to Bryan. He asked, "Are we to have our children know nothing about science except what the church says they shall know?" Malone said that the prosecution had argued the case was not about religion. He continued, "I defy anybody, after Mr. Bryan's speech, to believe that this was not a religious question."

After Bryan's hour-long speech defending the Butler Act, defense attorney Dudley Field Malone responded by challenging Bryan's argument.

Malone said the defense did not want to take away anyone's Bible or force them to give up their faith. But he wanted the fundamentalists to keep their Bible "in the world of theology, where it belongs and do not try to tell an intelligent world . . . that these books [of the Bible] . . . can be put into a course of science." Malone then asserted that the trial was about truth: "We are ready to tell the truth as we understand it. And we do not fear all the truth that they [the prosecutors] can present as facts. We are ready. We feel we stand with progress. We feel we stand with science. We feel we stand with intelligence. We feel we stand with fundamental freedom in America. We are not afraid. Where is the fear? We defy it!"

The courtroom, filled mostly with Tennesseans who supported Bryan, then erupted in cheers. H. L. Mencken wrote it was "a cheer at least four times as hearty as that given to Bryan. For these rustics delight in speechifying, and know when it is good." The people in the court enjoyed the flow of words and Malone's emotion—even if they still rejected evolution.

But the crowd's reaction did not influence Raulston. Several days later he ruled that the defense could not bring expert witnesses to discuss evolution and the evidence for it. The judge said that "the evidence of experts would shed no light on the issues." To Raulston the issues were as follows: Did the state have the power to pass the Butler Act? And did Scopes violate it? To him, the answer to both was clearly yes.

To some observers of the trial Scopes's case seemed doomed. Journalists began leaving Dayton. But those who did missed the real battle of words between Darrow and Bryan, between science and religion, still to come.

Four

Darrow Versus Bryan

WITH RAULSTON'S DECISION, the first week of the trial ended. Scopes later wrote that "Darrow had come to Dayton to confront Bryan. Now it seemed he would be denied the pleasure of courtroom combat." Over the weekend Darrow taunted Bryan a bit. Before the trial, Darrow said, Bryan had looked forward to openly challenging evolution in a "battle to the death." Now, Darrow said, by opposing the expert testimony, Bryan "has fled from the field, his forces disorganized." Bryan, for his part, told a crowd that agnostics and atheists were out to destroy Christianity. Meanwhile, on Sunday, Darrow prepared for a surprise move back in court.

On Monday morning, crowds once again stuffed the courthouse. Most people realized that the trial was almost over and wanted to hear the closing arguments. First, though, the defense was allowed to read some statements from the scientific experts and modernist theologians who had not been allowed to testify in court.

Bryan Takes the Stand

In the afternoon Raulston decided to move the trial to the speakers' platform in the center of town. Some people had

Darrow's Legal Problems

Clarence Darrow started July 20 with his own legal troubles. The previous Friday, he and Judge Raulston had argued over Darrow's request for more time to prepare witness statements. Darrow shouted and insulted the judge. On Monday morning Raulston ruled that Darrow was in contempt, meaning he had wrongly defied the court. Darrow would receive a sentence for his act the next day. After the break for lunch that day, Darrow apologized for his words. Raulston then replied, "The Man who died on the cross [Jesus Christ] that man might be redeemed, taught that it was godly to forgive, and were it not for the forgiving nature of God Himself I would fear for man. . . . I accept . . . Darrow's apology." The two men then shook hands, and the charge against Darrow was dropped.

suggested that the courthouse floor might collapse because of all the people jammed inside. Raulston also wanted as many people as possible to hear what would likely be the end of the trial. (The loudspeakers used earlier to broadcast to the crowds outside the courthouse had been taken away.)

The crowd soon grew to about three thousand people. Some sat on wooden benches, while others sought the shade of trees to avoid the blistering July sun. The crowd then heard Hays request that William Jennings Bryan be called to testify as an expert witness on religion. The judges and prosecutors were stunned—a defense lawyer calling the prosecutor of a case to testify was unheard of. The other lawyers protested and told Bryan not to do it. Judge Raulston asked Darrow if it was necessary. Darrow said that the case was about the conflict between evolution and religion. Earlier in the trial one scientific expert had been allowed to speak, and he had defined evolution. Now Darrow thought the jurors should hear a definition of religion. Bryan was eager for the chance, and Raulston finally agreed to the defense's unusual request. The part of the *Scopes* trial most people remember today was about to begin. For two hours Darrow defended reason and science while Bryan defended God and the Bible.

Bryan did not call himself an expert, but he said that he had studied the Bible for more than fifty years and often wrote about it. Darrow asked him if every word in the Bible was literally true. Bryan did not go that far—he knew some expressions and stories were metaphors. But he allowed that miracles could happen, such as the ones described in the Bible.

Darrow tried to show how some miracles contradicted scientific fact. The book of Joshua says Joshua commanded

This high-angle view captures Clarence Darrow (standing at right) questioning Bryan (seated at left with fan) during the trial.

the Sun to stand still, so the day would be longer. Yet that was impossible, since the Sun does not move around Earth; the planet moves around the Sun. Bryan said he knew which revolved around the other. So, Darrow asked, does that mean Earth would have to have been stopped to lengthen the day? Bryan said yes. Darrow then explained that if Earth had stopped, the planet would have been turned into "a molten mass of matter." Bryan said he did not know that for a fact, since he had never considered the notion. Darrow went on to talk about the biblical flood. The two men then discussed the possible date of the flood and the creation of Earth, with Bryan generally accepting that both had taken place between five thousand and six thousand years earlier. Darrow pointed out that most scientists believed humans were much older than that. Bryan did allow that not everything in the Bible was to be taken literally. During the act of creation, a day might not have been a twenty-four-hour day, but actually a longer period of millions of years.

Darrow continued, trying to show that Bryan was ignorant of basic facts of science and history. It appeared Bryan was not even curious about the world around him or other peoples and their civilizations. To that Bryan answered, "I have been so well satisfied with the Christian religion that I have spent no time trying to find arguments against it."

Reporting on the questioning, the *New York Times* described the "helplessness of the believer [Bryan] come so suddenly . . . on a moment when he could not reconcile statements of the Bible with generally accepted facts." This was Darrow's intent. Through Bryan, he wanted to attack literal views of the Bible, especially when such views were placed above science and reason. Bryan tried to defend his faith, and at times he drew applause from the crowd. But in the end most reporters believed Darrow had won the battle. Darrow claimed that afterward, "A friendly crowd followed me toward my home. Mr. Bryan left the grounds practically alone."

The Verdict

The next day Judge Raulston announced that he wanted Bryan's testimony from Monday removed from the court record. "The issue now is whether or not Mr. Scopes taught that man descended from a lower order of animals." Raulston believed that Bryan and Darrow's debate about God, creation, and the literal interpretation of the Bible did not matter. Darrow then admitted that the defense had no evidence or witnesses that could prove Scopes had not violated the law. He asked the judge to bring in the jury and to find Scopes guilty — which is what the ACLU and Darrow wanted all along.

The jury took just nine minutes to reach its "guilty" verdict. It then asked Raulston to set the fine for Scopes. Under Tennessee law the jury was supposed to do this, but Darrow agreed to let the judge set the sentence. Raulston fined the young teacher one hundred dollars. Scopes made a brief statement, the first time he spoke during the trial. He called the Butler Act unjust and said he would continue to oppose

John T. Scopes receives his sentence of a one-hundred-dollar fine from Judge Raulston for violating the Butler Act.

The Great Dayton Debate

The two-hour debate between Clarence Darrow and
William Jennings Bryan often drew strong reactions
from the crowd. In this excerpt both Darrow and
Bryan focus on the audience:

> Bryan: These gentlemen . . . did not come here to
> try this case. They came here to try revealed
> religion. I am here to defend it, and they can ask
> me any question they please.
>
> Raulston: All right. [Applause from the crowd]
>
> Darrow: Great applause from the bleachers!
>
> Bryan: From those whom you call "yokels."
>
> Darrow: I have never called them "yokels."

Bryan: That is, the ignorance of Tennessee, the bigotry.

Darrow: You mean who are applauding you?

Bryan: Those are the people whom you insult.

Darrow: You insult every man of science and learning in the world because he does not believe in your fool religion. . . .

Bryan: I am simply trying to protect the Word of God against the greatest atheist or agnostic in the United States. . . . [Prolonged applause] I want the world to know that agnosticism is trying to force agnosticism on our colleges and our schools, and the people of Tennessee will not permit that to be done.

it. He said, "Any other action would be in violation of my ideals of academic freedom." After a few statements from several of the lawyers and one final prayer, the trial of the century was over.

With the verdict in, both sides offered their opinions. The prosecutors had clearly won the legal battle. But the defense team and modernists thought they had gained something, too, by showing the intellectual weakness of fundamentalist thought. Some newspapers and magazines, though, thought neither side truly won. Bryan had come across as dumb, or as clearly not as smart as his opponent. Darrow, though, had struck some people as mean. Neither man's performance likely won him new fans, though old supporters cheered the lawyers' efforts.

The *Chicago Tribune* suggested the larger issue was not settled: "We'll not without a fight have the public school system of the United States supporting Mr. Bryan's beliefs with the public money, the courts, and the police." Bryan had tried to argue that a majority should not have to pay for the teachings of ideas they rejected, such as evolution. The *Tribune* and others flipped the issue around: people who rejected fundamentalism should not have to accept the teaching of creationist ideas, even if they were outnumbered—especially with the Constitution's guarantee of the separation of church and state.

H. L. Mencken had another concern. He wrote that he saw great ignorance on display in Dayton, even from the judge, a supposedly intelligent man. In his usual way, Mencken harshly called the people of Dayton and other fundamentalists morons, boobs, and yokels. He said the average person didn't have the knowledge or schooling to understand much of modern science, including evolution.

As science had progressed, he argued, "man in general has lagged far behind."

Out of the courtroom Bryan and Darrow continued their debate. Bryan released a statement. He said he was glad Christians now realized the nature of the "attacks which have been made, under cover of a scientific hypothesis, upon the authority of the Bible by unbelievers of every grade and class." Darrow responded, in part: "I have never tried to impose my view of religion on any human being that ever lived. I have a right to my own views and would fight as hard to protect every other man's views as I would fight to protect my own."

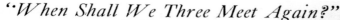

"When Shall We Three Meet Again?"

William Jennings Bryan (left) and Clarence Darrow (right) are satirized in this 1925 political cartoon shortly after the close of the Scopes Monkey Trial.

Five

Religion, Science, and Darwin

THE SCOPES TRIAL BROUGHT NATIONAL attention to a small-town schoolteacher. It gave two powerful personalities, Darrow and Bryan, a stage to present their opposing views. But decades of history and ideas led to their coming together in the Dayton courthouse. And the presence of one man was felt throughout the trial and during the ongoing debate between science and fundamentalism: Charles Darwin.

Faith and Science

Darwin, born in 1809, came from a scientific family. His father was a doctor, and his grandfather Erasmus had presented early ideas about evolution. But as a young man Darwin briefly planned to become a minister, assuming he would still have plenty of free time to pursue his hobby of studying nature.

With his scientific curiosity and his planned career as a minister, Darwin knew about the arguments developing in scholarly circles. Natural history and the general study of humans and the universe was giving way to more specialized scientific study. Scientists tried to balance what they observed in nature with Christian teachings about the world. One thinker concerned with both science and religion was

British naturalist Charles Darwin developed the theory of natural selection.

the theologian William Paley. He was what is now called a creationist. Paley believed, as did Bryan and the modern fundamentalists, that God created everything in the universe. In 1802 Paley argued that when examining a watch, a person immediately recognizes that someone designed its complicated parts to work as they do. Plants and animals, Paley said, had a similar or even greater complexity, which meant a skilled designer also created them. The designer, Paley said, was God.

A Young Earth?

The natural historians of Darwin's youth believed that Earth and the life on it were relatively young. An Anglican minister named James Ussher studied the events recorded in the Bible and calculated that Earth had been created in 4004 BCE. Some Christians might have argued over the exact date, but throughout the eighteenth century they generally agreed that God had created the universe fairly recently. By the nineteenth century scientists began to challenge some of the ideas of the creationists. In particular, the study of layers of rock and the discovery of fossils led some geologists to believe Earth was much older than Ussher and other Christians claimed. More likely, the planet had been created millions of years ago, not less than ten thousand years ago. Today, Christians who still believe that Earth is not several billions of years old, as scientists now say, are called young-Earth creationists.

Not all Christians welcomed the work of Paley and other scientists. Some Protestants of the time, called evangelicals, thought that scientific study, even if it honored God's role as creator, took humans' attention away from the spiritual world. Science promoted materialism and therefore could not be trusted. Other evangelicals simply ignored the new scientific theories, while some hoped the study of nature and biblical teachings could somehow mesh. Still, the split between Christians who saw the value of science and the wary evangelicals deepened as theories of evolution developed.

Creationism Challenged

Unlike some of the defenders of John Scopes, many of the early-nineteenth-century thinkers debating creationism and evolution were Christians. They were not trying to challenge religious authority. They simply wanted to present the facts of the natural world as they saw them. Some scientists hoped to prove that the new theories did not reject God's role as creator or his ongoing involvement in human life.

Darwin knew that new evidence suggested Earth was older than Christian thinkers thought and that scientists believed life forms evolved over time. He beleived that neither of these ideas directly challenged the role of God as creator. An older Earth did not mean God was not involved in its creation. And God could have set in motion the processes that led an early species to change into another. He also could have wiped out almost all living things with a flood, as described in the Bible, and then repopulated the planet with new plants and animals. God's design for Earth could have taken many forms, some scientists said. Yet some Christians rejected the new theories, especially evolution.

They believed all the species that ever lived were created by God at the same time, as the book of Genesis describes.

Darwin and Evolution

By the time he left college in 1831, Darwin was a skilled naturalist. Later that year he sailed on the English ship HMS *Beagle* on a voyage to South America. The trip would last for five years as the ship circled the globe. At some stops Darwin collected samples of local plants and animals and studied the terrain. He saw animals unknown to Europeans and noted the way earthquakes change the surface of Earth. On the Galapagos Islands, west of Ecuador, he saw that species of tortoises and some birds varied greatly from one island to another.

Back in England, Darwin talked to other scientists and pored over his notes. He also considered what he knew about fossils and the ideas of evolution circulating around Europe. Darwin was convinced that evolution happened and that humans had links to other animals. They had common ancestors. He could not prove that link, but he would spend several decades researching ideas on evolution. Further, he concluded that evolution was carried out by a process he called natural selection.

In a specific area, Darwin thought, the members of a particular species might compete for food or space. Some members have traits that help them adapt to their environment and survive. Other members lack these traits and therefore are more likely to die off. The members better suited to their environment are more likely to have offspring with the same helpful trait. Over time, more of the offspring with the useful trait survive. Through the passing

In 1871 the satirical magazine *The Hornet* published this caricature of Charles Darwin.

of the desirable traits from one generation to the next, nature "chooses" which members survive and how a species evolves. At times evolution leads to the creation of a new, separate species. These changes usually take place over a long period of time—perhaps millions of years.

In 1859 Darwin published his ideas in *On the Origin of Species*. He saw evolution as the gradual branching off of different species, traceable to a common ancestor. Variation and natural selection, he said, are the processes that make evolution happen. Darwin knew that his scientific conclusions were leading to the notion of a universe without a divine creator. "The old argument of design in nature," he wrote later in his life, "which formerly seemed to me so conclusive, fails, now that the law of natural selection has been discovered." But not everyone was ready or willing to accept Darwin's dismissal of God or to accept natural selection.

First Battles over Evolution

Adam Sedgwick had been one of Darwin's early teachers. He told Darwin that he read parts of Darwin's book with "absolute sorrow; because I think them utterly false & grievously mischievous. . . . Many of your wide conclusions are based upon assumptions which can neither be proved nor disproved." With the notion of natural selection, Sedgwick believed, Darwin was removing the idea of a link between God and nature. Destroying that link, Sedgwick said, would "sink the human race into a lower grade of degradation than any into which it has fallen since its written records tell us of its history." During the 1920s William Jennings Bryan would echo this idea during his battle to outlaw the teaching of evolution.

As Darwin expected, some religious thinkers also attacked his ideas. One was Samuel Wilberforce, an Anglican bishop. Unable to accept the idea of evolution in general, he said that "such a notion is absolutely incompatible . . . with single expressions in the word of God." This view would become common among American fundamentalists, who opposed any theory of creation that conflicted with the Bible. Yet other religious figures admired Darwin's work. Charles Kingsley, an Anglican minister and a naturalist, saw the possibility of God's giving creatures the ability to evolve over time. Yet Darwin had not meant to suggest this, since he saw nature itself, not God, as the driving force behind natural selection.

The debates about Darwinism moved into new magazines that were spreading across England. Among educated Protestant ministers and most scientists, the concept of evolution over long periods of time seemed plausible. By the end of the nineteenth century these thinkers largely rejected the idea of a "young Earth" that was only several thousand years old. They accepted the idea that Earth had been around for the millions of years needed to allow species evolve over time.

Still, the idea of natural selection remained unpopular and was not supported by the known science of the time. To many Christian scientists, natural selection was too random; Darwin seemed to suggest that nature went through a long process of trial and error as species developed variations over time. Only some of these variations were helpful to the species. These scientists still believed there had to be a greater design, or purpose, to evolution. They sometimes equated Darwinism with their own version of evolution while leaving out a key part of Darwin's idea—that evolution happened through the process of natural selection.

The Eclipse of Darwin

By the end of the nineteenth century many scientists and educated people were still uncomfortable with the idea of natural selection. The core of Darwin's theory openly rejected

Of Bishops and Apes

One of Darwin's earliest public defenders was Thomas Henry Huxley. Trained in zoology, he and Darwin often traded ideas on science. In 1860 Huxley had a famous public battle with Samuel Wilberforce. The exact words the two exchanged were not recorded, but Wilberforce supposedly asked Huxley if he had descended from apes on his grandmother's side or his grandfather's side. Huxley said he would rather "have a miserable ape for a grandfather" than someone like Wilberforce. Some in the audience later claimed that Huxley had said he'd rather be a monkey than a bishop. Historians think the tale is more legend than fact. But the story became popular, as Huxley and others saw themselves in conflict with religious thinkers who attacked the pursuit of scientific truth. The *Scopes* trial, and its battle between Clarence Darrow and William Jennings Bryan, is sometimes seen as the second round of the alleged Wilberforce-Huxley debate, pitting evolution against creationism.

God's role in creating new species. Christian thinkers turned to an older form of evolutionary theory that said animals could improve themselves on their own. Then they could pass on the new traits they had acquired. These ideas came from the eighteenth-century French biologist Jean-Baptiste Lamarck and were called Lamarckism. Though people at the turn of the nineteenth century often called evolution Darwinism, many were actually discussing Lamarckian ideas. Lamarck, unlike Darwin, created a theory of evolution that more Christians could accept. And Lamarck's theory did not put struggle or survival of the fittest at its center.

Lamarckian ideas led to what one historian called the eclipse of Darwin. His ideas were blocked out as thinkers tried to keep science and religion at least partially united. Yet some religious leaders remained suspicious of all theories of evolution.

During the 1910s American Protestants remained split on their views of evolution. The fundamentalists led the charge against Darwin and the teaching of his ideas in schools, which set the stage for the *Scopes* trial. This effort was part of a broader struggle to resist a new movement in religious thought, modernism.

The modernists saw that scientists mostly accepted evolution, even if they did not accept Darwin's ideas on natural selection. The modernists also knew about work in psychology and anthropology that placed religion in a cultural context. All peoples had the impulse to explain creation, life, and death through spiritual or supernatural forces. Modernist ministers and scholars also knew about a new way of examining the Bible, which said it should be judged according to known historical facts and the social conditions during

Catholics and Darwin

In both Darwin's time and today, most of the religious attacks against evolution and natural selection have come from fundamentalist Protestants. They, more than other Christians, have stressed that every word of the Bible is true and should shape human actions.

The Roman Catholic Church has more members in the United States than any other denomination. Church officials did not make any official statements about Darwin, but they tried to stop the writings of Catholic thinkers who supported him. Over time, however, the church began to accept the notion that the development of humans and other life forms might have been a natural process, but that a person's soul came from God.

Over time however, the church became increasingly comfortable with new evidence supporting Darwin's ideas. Today, Catholic leaders support the scientific truth of evolution and natural selection. They warn, however, that supporters should not try to make it a secular religion that replaces faith in God.

the times in which it was written. Using those standards, modernists realized that the facts disputed some of the teachings in the Bible. Yet the modernists still believed a person could accept that the Bible was inspired by God and would be a positive influence in modern life. In 1925 the ideas of the modernists led George Rappleyea to call together Dayton's leaders and challenge Tennessee's Butler Act. The verdict of the *Scopes* trial, however, seemed to show that modernist thinking was still unwelcome in Tennessee.

Six

The Next Legal Battles

THE BROADER QUESTION LEADING UP to the *Scopes* trial sometimes entered the Dayton courthouse in small ways. The defense called to mind previous battles between science and faith. Bryan defended the position of the creationists and stated the dangers of modernism. Yet as the prosecution argued, the case was really about one thing: had John T. Scopes violated the Butler Act? He had, and the broader issues, though discussed, did not decide the case.

Still, Bryan hoped to have one last chance to state his case for Christianity and against evolution. He had prepared a 15,000-word speech. The trial's quick end, however, prevented him from delivering it. Instead, after July 21, 1925, Bryan stayed in the Dayton area and gave parts of the speech. He planned to publish it and then deliver it across the country as a continuation of his antievolution crusade. But on July 26 Bryan died in Dayton while he slept. Some people claimed the public battering he took during the trial had played a role in his death. But Bryan's health had been poor for some time, as he suffered from diabetes. The heat and the stress of the trial may have aggravated his health problems, but Darrow's attacks did not kill the Great Commoner.

Honoring Bryan

After William Jennings Bryan's death, his body was taken by train from Dayton to Washington, D.C. At most stops people went to the station to see Bryan's coffin and pay their respects to a man they considered a hero. Once the coffin reached the nation's capital, another 20,000 people went to the church to honor Bryan. Fundamentalists particularly praised his efforts in the *Scopes* trial. Several singers recorded songs describing the court battle. One went: "He fought the evolutionists . . . fools / Who are trying to ruin the minds of children in our schools."

Before his death Bryan hoped that a Christian school would be built in Dayton to teach the fundamentalists' view of the world. By 1930 William Jennings Bryan University was opened for that purpose. Today it is known as Bryan College, and each year it holds a restaging of the *Scopes* trial, using actors to play Bryan and the other participants.

Appealing the *Scopes* Trial Verdict

Darrow spoke kindly of his *Scopes* trial foe. "I differed from him on many questions but always respected his sincerity and devotion." But Darrow had other concerns. He and the ACLU were preparing to appeal Scopes's case to the Tennessee Supreme Court. The case did not reach that higher court until mid–1926, and the decision came down the following January.

In *Scopes v. Tennessee* the state supreme court ruled that the Butler Act was constitutional. It addressed Darrow's concerns about the separation of church and state: "So far as we know, the denial or affirmation of such a theory [evolution] does not enter into any recognized mode of worship. . . . Belief or unbelief in the theory of evolution is no more a

William Jennings Bryan (right) died soon after the *Scopes* trial. Attorney Clarence Darrow (left) expressed his respect of his foe during the trial.

characteristic of any religious establishment or mode of worship than is belief or unbelief in the wisdom of the prohibition laws. It would appear that members of the same churches quite generally disagree as to these things."

The justices, however, did see a problem with the *Scopes* trial. Judge Raulston had improperly set the fine instead of letting the jury do it. On that ground they threw out the case. The state decided it would not pursue the issue any further. The ACLU no longer had a case to appeal to the U.S. Supreme Court, as it had hoped it would when it first sought a teacher to challenge the Butler Act.

The court's decision meant the Butler Act remained legal in Tennessee. Even before that decision Mississippi had passed a similar law, and Arkansas had passed one in 1928. Other states considered antievolution laws, but they failed to be passed. Still, the *Scopes* trial had a far-reaching effect. State lawmakers did not have to forbid the teaching of evolution. Acting on their own, local school districts began to remove it from their biology classes. So did textbook publishers. A new edition of Hunter's *Civic Biology* came out in 1927. It did not directly name the theory of evolution and did not discuss it as fully as the earlier edition did. For the next several decades Darwin and evolution largely disappeared from many U.S. schools.

Scientific Support Grows

Darwin's theories may have left the classroom, but scientists were finding more evidence to support them, especially the idea of natural selection. Paleontologists continued to find fossils that filled in the gaps between the different stages of human evolution. And geneticists began to explain how useful changes occurred during a species's evolution.

Genes contain the chemical codes that pass on traits from parents to offspring. Several genes combine to control one or more traits. A change in the chemicals—a mutation— can create a slight variation in the trait passed on. If the variation is helpful to a plant or animal's survival, it spreads through future generations. The parents with the positive trait are more likely to live and to have more offspring than members of the species without it. Mathematical models helped scientists see how the variations could spread across a population over time. In general the mutations, variations, and natural selection helped a certain species adapt to its environment. The science that drew on Darwin's ideas but was updated to address the new research was sometimes called neo-Darwinism.

In the 1950s scientists were getting an even better picture of how humans evolved. In the distant past—millions of years ago—humans and apes took different evolutionary paths. Together, modern humans, apes, monkeys, lemurs, and several related animals are known as primates. Humans evolved from ancient primates that lived in Africa. Those ancient primates walked on two legs and had much smaller brains than modern humans. Over time the primates evolved larger brains and learned how to use tools. Modern humans, called *Homo sapiens*, first appeared about 120,000 years ago.

The new findings led most scientists to believe what Darwin had: there was no driving force behind evolution whose goal was perfection in a species or the achievement of some moral goal. The purpose of evolution was survival. For some scientists this again led to a materialist viewpoint that left no room for God in creation. Yet some of the neo-Darwinists did remain Christian, if they had been previously. Others may have rejected God but still believed humans

By the 1950s scientists believed that some ancient primates from Africa evolved into the human species.

were destined to improve their actions and culture as the species evolved. As with the introduction of Darwin's theory in 1859, not everyone saw the issue as black-and-white—God and purpose versus no god and no purpose.

Evolution in the Classroom and the Court

As scientists found more evidence to support Darwin's theory, the teaching of evolution slowly increased. A survey taken in 1940 showed that more than half of the high school biology teachers who responded taught evolution. Some of them, however, admitted avoiding the subject of human evolution. In future surveys the number slowly increased, though

The Monkey Trial on Stage and Screen

In 1955 the play *Inherit the Wind* was staged in New York. The playwrights wrote a fictional version of the *Scopes* trial, but everyone knew which characters were based on Bryan, Darrow, Scopes, and the others involved in the trial. The play was not concerned with evolution as much as with the effort during the 1950s to fight communism, a political system in opposition to the democratic system practiced in the United States. The anti-communists sometimes seemed to be opponents of academic and intellectual freedom, as the fundamentalists had been during the 1920s. In the play and movie the Darrow figure is seen as the hero and Scopes as an innocent victim. The Bryan character is shown as a narrow-minded man who opposes all science—a distortion of Bryan's actual views. The movie helped create an image of the *Scopes* trial that most historians argue is false and unfair to Bryan.

teachers in southern states remained less likely to teach human evolution. Other teachers across the country said they spent only a small amount of time on the subject.

An event in 1957 brought new attention to the state of science in U.S. schools. That year the Soviet Union launched *Sputnik*, the first artificial satellite. The United States and the Soviet Union were military rivals, and some Americans worried that the Soviets were ahead in the race to develop new, more powerful weapons. The U.S. government began to push for more rigorous science education in order to produce more scientists. University professors began to study the textbooks used in high schools and were surprised to find that evolution was barely mentioned. New textbooks that made evolution a key part of understanding biology began appearing in 1963. When these first books sold well, more publishers printed texts that explained the role of evolution in great detail. School officials faced pressure from parents to teach the more modern views on science.

By this time Tennessee, Arkansas, and Mississippi still had laws that prohibited the teaching of evolution, though they were rarely enforced. Some science teachers in those states wanted to repeal the laws and openly called for the teaching of evolution. In 1965 Arkansas introduced a new textbook that described Darwinian evolution. A tenth-grade science teacher, Susan Epperson, decided to challenge the law that made it illegal for her to teach that subject. Two years later Tennessee biology teacher Gary L. Scott filed a lawsuit after he was fired for teaching evolution and calling the Bible "a bunch of fairy tales."

Both cases received national attention and were sometimes referred to as Scopes II. Scott dropped his suit after Tennessee lawmakers voted to repeal the Butler Act.

Arkansas science teacher Susan Epperson supported the teaching of evolution and challenged the state's anti-evolution law in 1965.

A Memphis newspaper sparked the repeal effort, and many Tennesseans did not want to stir up the memories of the 1925 Monkey Trial. The state senate needed two votes to repeal the law. Some fundamentalist senators, however, still wanted to use the Bible as the supreme source for explaining creation. The threat of another *Scopes* trial, with the negative national attention it would draw, finally led the senate to repeal the Butler Act.

Susan Epperson's case did reach the courts, and it went all the way to the U.S. Supreme Court. Once again the ACLU supported educators' right to teach evolution, as they focused on the First Amendment. The Arkansas law, which was similar to the Butler Act, denied Epperson her right to free speech by preventing her from teaching Darwinian evolution. The law also favored the views of one religious group—fundamentalist Protestants—over the views of others. One Arkansas court supported Epperson, but the state supreme court overturned that decision. That court said Arkansas had the right to decide what was taught in its schools and did not rule on the constitutional issues Epperson raised.

In November 1968 the U.S. Supreme Court decided *Epperson v. Arkansas*. In previous cases the court had ruled that the Fourteenth Amendment applied to the Bill of Rights. This meant states could not violate the rights spelled out in the first ten amendments to the U.S. Constitution. Justice Abe Fortas, writing for the court, said the Arkansas law clearly violated the Constitution: "There is and can be no doubt that the First Amendment does not permit the State to require that teaching and learning must be tailored to the principles or prohibitions of any religious sect." The ruling meant no state could pass a law, for religious purposes, that punished the teaching of Darwinian evolution. But as with the *Scopes* trial, a legal decision did not settle the issue.

Seven

A Continuing Debate

MODERNISTS AND DARWINISTS WELCOMED the *Epperson* decision. Most fundamentalists, however, wanted to keep battling against the teaching of evolution in public schools. Even before *Epperson* was decided, a new movement had begun in fundamentalist circles. It laid the foundation for what became known as creation science.

In 1961 Henry M. Morris and John Whitcomb wrote a book called *The Genesis Flood*. Morris was an engineer, and Whitcomb was a theologian. The two authors argued that Earth's current geological state could be traced back to the great flood described in the Bible. They were literalists, believing that God created everything in six normal days and that Earth was young—thousands, not billions, of years old. Mixing science and religion, *The Genesis Flood* argued that evolution could not have occurred as Darwin and his followers described.

Morris claimed that the biblical flood left behind the fossils scientists used to plot the evolution of various species. To Morris, all the life forms existed at the same time, until the flood wiped out everything except Noah and the animals he carried on his ark.

In 1963 Morris and other Christian scientists formed the Creation Research Society (CRS) to promote young-Earth science and to fight the teaching of evolution. All members had to sign a statement that included this: "All basic types of living things, including man, were made by direct creative acts of God during the Creation Week described in Genesis." The CRS published a science textbook promoting creation science. Morris later published his own, in two editions. The one meant for private, Christian schools listed direct references to the Bible, while the one meant for public schools did not. Still, it was clear Morris based his general ideas on a literal reading of Genesis, as creationists had hundreds of years earlier. In 1970 Morris founded the Institute for Creation Research (ICR) to seek scientific evidence for a Bible-based theory of creation.

Another Legal Battle

Morris's works and the writings of other creation scientists appealed to American fundamentalists but did not have much impact in most public schools. Most scientists and teachers still believed neo-Darwinian evolution was the correct explanation of how life developed on Earth. So the ICR and other creationist groups decided to enter the political arena to promote their cause. Fundamentalists began asking local school boards to teach creationism alongside Darwinian evolution. They argued that the two should be presented as equally possible explanations for how life formed on Earth.

By the early 1980s the fundamentalists were asking state governments to give the two theories equal time in the classroom. Lawmakers in twenty-seven states considered such a law, but those in only two — Arkansas and Louisiana — passed

Debating Creation Science

In 1981 Henry M. Morris publicly debated with a scientist who favored Darwin's theories. Morris met Ken Miller of Brown University in Providence, Rhode Island, at that school, in front of a packed house of 1,600 people. By most accounts, Miller, a Roman Catholic, "won" the debate, and Morris did admit that Miller was the most skilled Darwinist he had faced. The two men met in public two more times. Miller later called Morris a polite, sincere Christian who "also was profoundly wrong in his views of science and Christianity." In later years Morris said that Miller was not a true Christian, since he did not accept the Bible as the literal word of God and never mentioned the importance of Jesus Christ. In reviewing a book Miller wrote, Morris said, "There is such overwhelming evidence for the truth of Biblical Christianity and such strong, confirming, scientific evidence for its worldview. To believe that God exists is nice, but it is not nice to charge that His revelation is false or misleading."

one. Both laws were immediately challenged by the ACLU. Though Morris and others called their views science, the ACLU and others said the fundamentalists were actually trying to teach their religious views as fact.

In the trial challenging the Arkansas law, experts were allowed to testify. Scientists and theologians agreed that creation science was religion and should not be taught in public schools. Defense experts disagreed. Unlike the *Scopes* case, the trial was heard in a federal court. The judge, relying on past rulings by the U.S. Supreme Court, said the Arkansas law violated the establishment clause of the First Amendment. This clause says government cannot favor one religion over another.

During the early 1980s some state governments considered passing laws that would allow the teaching of creationism and Darwinian evolution.

Louisiana lawmakers had tried to write their equal-time law so it would survive a court challenge. The law did not use words from the Bible to define creation science. And the law said creation science had to be taught only if evolution was taught. Schools could choose to teach neither. Still, teachers and parents joined together to sue the state, seeking to have the so-called Creationism Act thrown out. Two federal courts ruled against the state, which appealed to the U.S. Supreme Court.

The case was called *Edwards v. Aguillard*, and as in *Epperson*, the court ruled against the anti-evolution forces. William Brennan, writing for the majority, said the Creationism Act violated the establishment clause. The law did not use biblical terms to define creationism, but the lawmakers who wrote it were clearly trying to promote their religious views. Brennan noted, "The lead witness at the hearings introducing the original bill, Luther Sunderland, described creation science as postulating [suggesting] 'that everything was created by some intelligence or power external to the universe.'" One lawmaker said that the existence of God was a scientific fact. Brennan also said the Louisiana law limited academic freedom by making the teaching of evolution reliant on teaching creation science.

Antonin Scalia was one of two justices who dissented from the majority. Scalia noted that one expert who spoke in favor of the law said hundreds of scientists accepted creation science. He also quoted one lawmaker who said he wanted to stop the "censoring" that occurred when textbook companies did not present creationism as a valid theory. That aim, Scalia said, was not religious, but an effort to air all sides of a genuine scientific debate. With that as the law's goal, it did not violate the establishment clause. He added, "We have no basis on the record to conclude that creation science need be anything other than a collection of scientific data supporting the theory that life abruptly appeared on earth. . . . [T]o posit [suggest] a past creator is not to posit the eternal and personal God who is the object of religious veneration [worship]."

The Rise of Intelligent Design

By the time the Supreme Court settled *Edwards v. Aguillard*, a new scientific theory was rising to challenge both creation science and neo-Darwinism. Starting in the mid–1980s, a group of scientists developed the notion of intelligent design (ID). The name called to mind the earlier idea of design that many ministers and scientists had championed in Darwin's lifetime. The ID writers suggested that parts of nature were too complex to have occurred by chance in nature.

The first book describing ID was *The Mystery of Life's Origin*. The book, written by a physical chemist and mechanical engineer and a geochemist, was backed by a fundamentalist Christian group. But the authors, and later ID supporters, did not use the Bible to explain creation. They also did not rule out the possibility that evolution or natural selection played a part in the development of species. Instead, while exploring the nature of genes and other complex aspects of biology, they argued that some intelligent force outside nature set the wheel of life in motion. They did not say it had to be God, but personally they believed God was the intelligent designer.

While ID satisfied some Christians, creationists still rejected it. John Whitcomb said, "The tragedy of the [ID] movement, however, is that it deliberately stops short of honoring God's written revelation on origins, the Bible. In fact, the book of Genesis as literal history seems to be an embarrassment and an unwanted and unnecessary burden to bear in the debate with evolution-oriented scientists."

Still, the ID movement received a boost in 1991 with Philip E. Johnson's *Darwin on Trial*. Johnson, a lawyer, argued that modern science did not prove Darwin's theory of natural selection. Darwinian theory, he said, rests on certain beliefs that cannot be proven, such as "The cosmos is a closed system of material causes and effects." Johnson added that the Darwinists wanted schools to teach the theory of evolution, "not . . . present fairly the evidence that is causing Darwinism so much trouble." He also criticized materialists for ruling out from the start that God or some other supernatural force could have played a role in the creation process.

In the years that followed, Christian scientists with academic backgrounds promoted different interpretations of ID. One of them was Michael J. Behe, a biochemist. In his 1996 book *Darwin's Black Box*, he explored new facts in his field that suggested biochemists did not understand the origins of proteins and other chemicals that control cells: "No one at Harvard University, no one at the National Institute of Health . . . no Nobel prize winner—no one at all can give a detailed account of how . . . any complex biochemical process might have developed in a Darwinian fashion." Behe argued that a designer was responsible for these complex systems. Some scientists, both materialists and believers in God, thought Behe made logical errors in his argument in an effort to attack evolutionary theory.

Some ID scientists have pointed out that many new ideas have been challenged as they first developed. William Dembski, a mathematician and philosopher, is a champion of ID. He wrote in 2004 that he and other ID "revolutionaries . . . must be willing to take the abuse, ridicule, and intimidation that the ruling elite can inflict. The ruling elite in this case are the dogmatic Darwinists and scientific naturalists."

Opponents of ID said that no matter how scientific ID seemed to be, the theory still rested on faith in God, rather than on observable facts, to explain creation. The ID supporters stuck to their belief that, as Dembski wrote, "There are natural systems that cannot be adequately explained in terms of undirected natural forces." The only explanation, he argued, is the role of someone or something that displays intelligence.

Dembski and Behe could not convince some Christian scientists to give up natural selection. Francis Collins, a geneticist and evangelical Protestant, spoke for many scientists who believe in both God and Darwinian evolution:

> The evidence for Darwin's theory of descent from a common ancestor by gradual change over long periods of time operated on by natural selection is absolutely overwhelming. . . . I'll give you the view that I've arrived at, which in my experience is also the view that about 40 percent of working scientists who believe in a personal God have arrived at. . . . God, who is not limited in space or time, created this universe 13.7 billion years ago with its parameters precisely tuned to allow the development of complexity over long periods of time. That plan included the mechanism of evolution to create this marvelous diversity of living things on our planet and to include ourselves, human beings.

ID in the Classroom

While individual ID scientists did not necessarily talk about the Christian God as the source of that intelligence, some fundamentalists did. They used ID books to launch another attempt to get Darwin out of the classroom. ID suggested there was a scientific explanation for creation that did not rest on materialism but did not directly mention God. Some fundamentalists thought introducing ID in schools would let them successfully win any legal challenges, such as the one creation science had lost. At the same time they could use ID to remove the atheistic tendencies they saw in neo-Darwinism.

The theory of intelligent design began to gain popularity by the mid–1980s. This theory stated that a scientific explanation of creation was evident. These students put together DNA models in their biology class in Santa Paula, California.

Following ideas based more on Henry Morris's than on those of Philip Johnson and other ID thinkers, Kansas creationists led the new attack on evolution. Johnson, though, supported the state's actions in 1999, when it changed the outline for what should be taught in biology. The new guidelines took out references to some evolutionary ideas, such as the age of Earth. Most scientists attacked the changes. Stephen Jay Gould, a strong supporter of evolution, said the Kansas action "marks the latest episode of a long struggle by religious fundamentalists and their allies to restrict or eliminate the teaching of evolution in public schools." He said the board's argument against evolution "smacks of absurdity and only reveals ignorance about the nature of science."

Still, in the years to come, Kansas and other states turned even more strongly against evolution and promoted ID. And as in the past the ACLU challenged the anti-evolutionists. In 2004 the Dover, Pennsylvania, school board voted to allow students access to an ID textbook, while noting that Darwinism was a theory that contained "gaps"—ideas with no evidence to support them. Working with local parents who opposed ID, the ACLU argued that ID was more religion than science and could not be taught.

The trial, *Kitzmiller v. Dover*, began in 2005. Experts testified on both sides. For ID, Michael Behe and others argued that ID was science. A theologian, however, said ID supporters basically made the same arguments religious figures had made for centuries regarding God's role in creation. Records showed that the publisher of the ID textbook used in Dover had sold the same book before the Supreme Court's 1987 decision in *Edwards*. Afterward, the publisher merely replaced the word *creationism* with *intelligent design*. Other than that change, the book was still centered on a religious view of creation. Looking over the testimony, federal judge John E. Jones III wrote, "We conclude that the religious nature of ID would be readily apparent to an objective observer, adult or child." Given that, Jones decided that the Dover school board had violated the establishment clause.

Not surprisingly, supporters of ID, such as the Discovery Institute, rejected the notion that ID and creationism should be judged in the same way. In 2006 the institute's Stephen C. Meyer wrote, "ID holds that there are tell-tale features of living systems and the universe that are best explained by a designing intelligence. The theory does not challenge the idea of evolution defined as change over time, or even common ancestry, but it disputes Darwin's idea that the cause of biological change is wholly blind and undirected. . . . ID may provide support for theistic belief. But that is not grounds for dismissing it."

The Fight Goes On

The *Kitzmiller* decision did not end efforts by Christians to weaken the presence of Darwin in the classroom. The Discovery Institute supports the idea of students' hearing all theories of creation when studying science. Texas passed such a standard in 2009. A spokesman from the institute said strict Darwinists unfairly opposed the teaching of any ideas that questioned Darwinian evolution: "Let's be absolutely clear: Under the new standards, students will be expected to analyze and evaluate the scientific evidence for evolution. . . ."

Meanwhile, most scientists have continued to call for teaching evolution without any reference to ID. In 2008 the National Academy of Sciences released a book exploring the most recent evidence for neo-Darwinist thought. The academy stated its basic view: "Given the importance of science in all aspects of modern life, the science curriculum should not be undermined with nonscientific material. Teaching creationist ideas in science classes confuses what constitutes science and what does not."

The academy's book came out just a few years after most Americans said they thought creationism should be taught in schools. That desire could be fueled by religious beliefs, the idea that Darwin's theory does have gaps, or both. On the other side, the ACLU and others continue to resist promoting one set of religious beliefs in public schools. Scientists themselves remain split. Some are strict materialists who oppose religion in all its forms. One spokesman for that view is Steven Weinberg, winner of a Nobel Prize in physics. He said in 1999, "One of the great achievements of science has been, if not to make it impossible for intelligent people to be religious, then at least to make it possible for them not to be religious. . . . Nature is governed by impersonal laws, laws that do not give any special status to life, and yet laws that humans are able to discover and understand."

Some Christians believe neo-Darwinism explains how life developed on Earth. Some religious scientists support creationism or ID. The search to explain how life formed and changes will continue. So will the legal battle over what should be taught in schools. The *Scopes* trial was just the beginning of the debate between science and religion in American life.

Timeline

November 1859 Charles Darwin publishes *On the Origin of Species*, which explains his theory of evolution based on natural selection.

June 1860 Scientist Thomas Henry Huxley defends Darwin's ideas in a debate with minister Samuel Wilberforce.

1910 Lyman Stewart begins publishing *The Fundamentals*, writings that defend traditional Christian beliefs.

1921 William Jennings Bryan starts to campaign against the teaching of evolution in public schools.

March 1925 The Butler Act takes effect in Tennessee, making it illegal to deny the biblical story of creation and to teach Darwinian evolution.

May 1925 John T. Scopes agrees to be arrested for violating the Butler Act so that its constitutionality can be challenged in court.

July 1925 The *Scopes* trial begins, with Clarence Darrow helping to defend Scopes and Bryan working for the prosecution. Scopes is found guilty of violating the Butler Act and is fined one hundred dollars.

January 1927 On an appeal of the *Scopes* trial verdict, the Tennessee Supreme Court rules that the Butler Act is constitutional, but it overturns Scopes's conviction.

January 1955 *Inherit the Wind*, loosely based on the *Scopes* trial, appears on Broadway in New York City.

1961   Henry M. Morris and John Whitcomb publish *The Genesis Flood*, which marks the beginning of modern creation science.

1963   Public schools begin using new textbooks that stress the theory of evolution.

November 1968   In *Epperson v. Arkansas* the U.S. Supreme Court overturns an Arkansas law prohibiting the teaching of Darwinian evolution.

June 1987   In *Edwards v. Aguillard* the U.S. Supreme Court rules that states cannot force schools to teach creationism and evolution as equally valid scientific theories.

June 1991   Philip E. Johnson publishes *Darwin on Trial*, which promotes the idea of intelligent design to explain the creation of life.

December 2005   In *Kitzmiller v. Dover* federal judge John E. Jones III rules that intelligent design is a form of religious belief and therefore cannot be taught in public schools.

Notes

Chapter One

p. 10, "The town was filled . . . duel to the death." John T. Scopes, quoted in "Monkey Trial," *American Experience*, <www.pbs.org/wgbh/amex/monkeytrial/filmmore/pt.html> (Accessed on 12 May 2009).

p. 11, "any theory . . . in the Bible." "Public Acts of the State of Tennessee," Famous Trials in American History: The Scopes Trial. <www.law.umkc.edu/faculty/projects/ftrials/scopes/tennstat.htm> (Accessed on 12 May 2009).

p. 13, "put Dayton on the map." Walter White, quoted in Edward J. Larson, *Summer for the Gods*. New York: Basic Books, 2006, p. 91.

p. 13, "Then you've been violating the law." Frank E. Robinson, quoted in *Summer for the Gods*, p. 90.

p. 14, "All thought . . . freedom of opinion." ACLU Statement of Purpose, quoted in Robert C. Cottrell, *Roger Nash Baldwin and the American Civil Liberties Union*. New York: Columbia University Press, 2000, p. 121.

p. 15, "is a supporter . . . in every form." Quoted in Cottrell, *Roger Nash Baldwin and the American Civil Liberties Union*, p. 133.

p. 16, "The Butler Act . . . rest of society." John T. Scopes, "Reflections 40 Years After." Excerpted at Famous Trials in American History: The Scopes Trial. <www.law.umkc.edu/faculty/projects/ftrials/scopes/scopesreflections.html> (Accessed on 1 June 2009).

p. 17, "to limit . . . after truth." John Randolph Neal, quoted in Larson, *Summer for the Gods*, p. 95.

p. 18, "instincts . . . Europe and America." George William Hunter, *A Civic Biology Presented in Problems*. New York: American Book Company, 1914, p. 196. Available online at <http://books.google.com/books?id=C8EXAAAAIAA J&dq=george+william+hunter+civic+biology&printsec= frontcover&source=bl&ots=qQsD6k6mbC&sig=LmNV XogemKHVhb62gEFCWdHLbdM&hl=en&ei=rpBTS u_aGZOEtweZ6JSbCA&sa=X&oi=book_result&ct= result&resnum=1> (Accessed on 1 June 2009).

Chapter Two

p. 24, "the natural tendency . . . faith in evolution." William Jennings Bryan, *The Menace of Darwinism*. New York: Fleming H. Revell Company, 1922, p. 4. Available online at <http://ia341013.us.archive.org/3/items/menaceofdarwin is00brya/menaceofdarwinis00brya.pdf> (Accessed on 28 May 2009).

p. 24, "While claiming . . . individuals?" Bryan, *The Menace of Darwinism*, p. 5.

p. 25, "atheism . . . the brutes." Bryan, quoted in Michael Kazin, *A Godly Hero: The Life of William Jennings Bryan*. New York: Anchor Books, 2006, p. 275.

p. 25. "revolt against modernity." Richard Hofstadter, *Anti-Intellectualism in American Life*. New York: Vintage Books, 1963, p. 117.

p. 26, "When Darwin . . . biology." Harry Emerson Fosdick, "Attacks W.J.B.: Preacher Says Bryan's Article on Evolution Works Injury to Bible." *New York Times*, 12 March 1922, p. 91.

p. 27, "the faith of men . . . the need of a Saviour." William Jennings Bryan, *In His Image*. Electronic version at Project Gutenberg, <www.gutenberg.org/files/12744/12744-8.txt> (Accessed on 12 May 2009).

p. 28, "the Good Book . . . against the monkeys." Roger Baldwin, quoted in Cottrell, *Roger Nash Baldwin*, p. 155.

p. 28, "At once I wanted . . . religious fanaticism." Clarence Darrow, *The Story of My Life*. Reprint. New York: Da Capo Press, 1996, p. 249.

p. 30, "a poor clod . . . inflaming half-wits." H. L. Mencken, *The Vintage Mencken*. Gathered by Alistair Cooke. New York: Vintage Books, 1955, pp. 164–165.

p. 31, "the trial would become a circus." John T. Scopes, quoted in Larson, *Summer for the Gods*, p. 102.

p. 32, READ YOUR BIBLE DAILY FOR ONE WEEK. Quoted in Marion Elizabeth Rodgers, *Mencken: The American Iconoclast*. New York: Oxford University Press, 2005, p. 276.

Chapter Three

p. 34, "that in a case . . . with prayer." Darrow, *The Story of My Life*, p. 259.

p. 35, "an effort on the part . . . have a right to do." Tom Stewart, quoted in Leslie H. Allen, ed., *Bryan and Darrow at Dayton: The Record and Documents of the "Bible Evolution Trial."* New York: Arthur Lee, 1925, p. 14.

p. 35, "makes the Bible . . . every man's learning." Darrow, quoted in Allen, *Bryan and Darrow*, p. 29.

p. 37, "the Tennesseans who . . . crushing force." "Decision

Today Is Likely; Judge Will Also Decide on Whether He Will Hear Scientists." *New York Times*, 14 July 1925, p. 1.

p. 37, "The eyes . . . are upon you here." Arthur Garfield Hays, quoted in Larson, *Summer for the Gods*, p. 176.

p. 37, "This is a court . . . at large." Herbert Hicks, quoted in Larson, *Summer for the Gods*, p. 176.

p. 37, "Do you believe the story of divine creation?" Ben McKenzie, quoted in Allen, *Bryan and Darrow*, p. 62.

p. 38, "That is none of your business." Arthur Garfield Hays, quoted in Allen, *Bryan and Darrow*, p. 62.

p. 38, "While the defense thinks . . . evolution and Christianity." Dudley Field Malone, quoted in Allen, *Bryan and Darrow*, p. 45.

p. 38, "And yet . . . as proved." William Jennings Bryan, quoted in Allen, *Bryan and Darrow*, pp. 72–73.

p. 40, "not listening . . . over the crowd." John T. Scopes, quoted in Robert A. Cherny, *A Righteous Cause: The Life of William Jennings Bryan*. Boston: Little, Brown and Company, 1985, p. 178.

p. 40, "Are we to have . . . they shall know?" Malone, quoted in Allen, *Bryan and Darrow*, p. 83.

p. 40, "I defy . . . a religious question." Malone, quoted in Allen, *Bryan and Darrow*, p. 84.

p. 41, "in the world . . . into a course of science." Malone, quoted in Allen, *Bryan and Darrow*, p. 86.

p. 41, "We are ready . . . We defy it!" Malone, quoted in Allen, *Bryan and Darrow*, p. 86.

p. 41, "a cheer at least . . . when it is good." H. L. Mencken, "Malone the Victor, Even Though Court Sides with

Opponents, Says Mencken," *Baltimore Evening Sun*, 17 July 1925. Available online at Positive Atheism <www.positiveatheism.org/hist/menck04.htm#SCOPES9> (Accessed on 3 June, 2009).

p. 41, "the evidence . . . on the issues." John Raulston, quoted in Allen, *Bryan and Darrow*, p. 93.

Chapter Four

p. 42, "Darrow had come . . . courtroom combat." John T. Scopes, quoted in "Monkey Trial." (Accessed on 3 June 2009).

p. 42, "has fled . . . disorganized." Clarence Darrow, quoted in Levine, *Defender of the Faith*, p. 346.

p. 43, "The Man who died . . . Darrow's apology." John T. Raulston, quoted in Allen, *Bryan and Darrow*, p. 111.

p. 45, "a molten mass of matter." Darrow, quoted in Allen, *Bryan and Darrow*, p. 138.

p. 46, "I have been . . . arguments against it." Bryan, quoted in Allen, *Bryan and Darrow*, p. 146.

p. 46, "helplessness of the believer . . . generally accepted facts." "Big Crowd Watches Trial Under Trees." *New York Times*, 21 July 1925, p. 1.

p. 46, "A friendly crowd . . . practically alone." Darrow, *The Story of My Life*, p. 267.

p. 46, "The issue now . . . order of animals." Raulston, quoted in Allen, *Bryan and Darrow*, p. 157.

p. 48, These gentlemen . . . will not permit that to be done." Bryan, Raulston, Darrow, quoted in Allen, *Bryan and Darrow*, pp. 139–140, 151.

p. 50, "Any other action . . . academic freedom." Scopes, quoted in Allen, *Bryan and Darrow*, p. 161.

p. 50, "We'll not . . . the police." "As Expected, Bryan Wins." *Chicago Tribune*, 22 July 1925, p. 8.

p. 51, "man in general has lagged far behind." H. L. Mencken, "Fundamentalism: Divine and Secular." *Chicago Tribune*, 20 September 1925, p. E1.

p. 51, "attacks which have been made . . . every grade and class." William Jennings Bryan, quoted in Allen, *Bryan and Darrow*, p. 165.

p. 51, "I have never . . . protect my own." Clarence Darrow, quoted in Allen, *Bryan and Darrow*, p. 168.

Chapter Five

p. 58, "The old argument . . . has been discovered." Darwin, *The Autobiography*, p. 73.

p. 58, "absolute sorrow . . . nor disproved." Adam Sedgwick, letter to Charles Darwin, 24 November 1859. Available online at The Darwin Correspondence Project, <www.darwinproject.ac.uk/darwinletters/calendar/entry-2548.html> (Accessed on 16 May 2009).

p. 58, "sink the . . . of its history." Sedgwick to Darwin, 24 November 1859.

p. 58, "such a notion . . . the word of God." Samuel Wilberforce, quoted in Janet Brown, *Charles Darwin: The Power of Place*. Princeton, NJ: Princeton University Press, 2002, p. 114.

p. 60, "have a miserable ape for a grandfather." Thomas Henry Huxley, quoted in Brown, *The Power of Place*, p. 122.

Chapter Six

p. 65, "He fought the evolutionists . . . in our schools." "Death of William Jennings Bryan," quoted in Larson, *Summer for the Gods*, p. 204.

p. 66, "I differed . . . sincerity and devotion." Darrow, quoted in Allen, *Bryan and Darrow*, p. 202.

p. 66, "So far as we know . . . to these things." Grafton Green, *John Thomas Scopes v. The State.* Famous Trials in American History: The Scopes Trial. <www.law.umkc.edu/faculty/projects/ftrials/scopes/statcase.htm> (Accessed on 6 June, 2009).

p. 71, "a bunch of fairy tales." Gary L. Scott, quoted in Larson, *Summer for the Gods*, p. 250.

p. 73, "There is . . . any religious sect." Abe Fortas, *Epperson v. Arkansas.* Available online at <http://supreme.justia.com/us/393/97/case.html> (Accessed on 8 June, 2009).

Chapter Seven

p. 75, "All basic types . . . described in Genesis." Creation Research Society Statement of Belief, quoted in Eugenie Scott, *Evolution vs. Creationism: An Introduction.* Berkeley: University of California Press, 2004, p. 100.

p. 76, "also was profoundly wrong . . . done damage." Ken Miller, quoted in Valerie J. Nelson, "Henry Morris, 87; 1961 Book Is Credited With Reviving the Creationism Movement." *Los Angeles Times*, 3 March 2006. Available online at <http://articles.latimes.com/2006/mar/03/local/me-morris3?pg=1> (Accessed on 23 June 2009).

p. 76, "There is such . . . false or misleading." Henry Morris, "Finding an Evolutionists's God." Institute for Creation Research, <www.icr.org/article/finding-evolutionists-god> (Accessed on 23 June 2009).

p. 78, "The lead witness . . . external to the universe." William Brennan, *Edwards v. Aguillard*. Available online at <http://supreme.justia.com/us/482/578/case.html> (Accessed on 24 June 2009).

p. 78, "We have no basis . . . religious veneration." Antonin Scalia, *Edwards v. Aguillard*. Available online at <http://supreme.justia.com/us/482/578/case.html> (Accessed on 24 June 2009).

p. 79, "The tragedy . . . evolution-oriented scientists." John C. Whitcomb, "The Intelligent Design Movement." Answers in Genesis.org, 21 September 2005. Available online at <www.answersingenesis.org/docs2005/0921whitcomb_pt2.asp> (Accessed on 25 June 2009).

p. 80, "The cosmos . . . so much trouble." Philip E. Johnson, *Darwin on Trial*. Washington, D.C.: Regnery Gateway, 1991, p. 144.

p. 80, "No one at Harvard . . . in a Darwinian fashion." Michael J. Behe, *Darwin's Black Box: The Biochemical Challenge to Evolution*. New York: Touchstone, 1996.

p. 80, "revolutionaries . . . Darwinists and scientific naturalists." William A. Dembski, *The Design Revolution: Answering the Toughest Questions About Intelligent Design*. Downers Grove, IL: InterVarsity Press, 2004, p. 20.

p. 81, "There are natural systems . . . natural forces." Dembski, *The Design Revolution*, p. 27.

p. 81, The evidence . . . human beings. Francis Collins, "Can Science and Religion Co-exist in Harmony?" Pew Research Center Publications, 22 June 2009. Available online at <http://pewresearch.org/pubs/1259/can-science-and-faith-be-reconciled> (Accessed on 25 June 2009).

p. 83, "marks the latest episode . . . nature of science." Stephen Jay Gould, quoted in Edward Larson and Larry Witham, "Inherit an Ill Wind." Famous Trials in American History: The Scopes Trial. <www.law.umkc.edu/faculty/projects/ftrials/scopes/tennstat.htm> (Accessed on 25 June 2009).

p. 84, "We conclude . . . adult or child." John E. Jones III, *Kitzmiller v. Dover*. Available online at The TalkOrigins Archive, <www.talkorigins.org/faqs/dover/kitzmiller_v_dover_decision.html> (Accessed on 25 June 2009).

p. 84, "ID holds . . . grounds for dismissing it." Stephen C. Meyer, "Intelligent Design Is Not Creationism." *Daily Telegraph*, 28 January 2006. Available online at <www.telegraph.co.uk/comment/personal-view/3622692/Intelligent-design-is-not-creationism.html> (Accessed on 25 June 2009).

p. 84, "Let's be absolutely clear . . . evidence for evolution." Discovery Institute, 27 March 2009. Available online at <www.discovery.org/a/9851> (Accessed on 25 June 2009).

p. 85, "Given the importance . . . and what does not." "Evolution and Creationism in Schools." The National Academies. <www.nationalacademies.org/evolution/InSchools.html> (Accessed on 25 June 2009).

p. 85, "One of the great achievements . . . discover and understand." Steven Weinberg, quoted in Douglas O. Linder, "Steven Weinberg on Religion and Science." Famous Trials in American History: The Scopes Trial. <www.law.umkc.edu/faculty/projects/ftrials/scopes/tennstat.htm> (Accessed on 15 May 2009).

Further Information

Books

Fitzgerald, Stephanie. *The Scopes Trial: The Battle over Teaching Evolution*. Minneapolis: Compass Point, 2007.

Fleisher, Paul. *Evolution*. Minneapolis: Lerner Publishing Group, 2006.

Fridell, Ron. *Religious Fundamentalism*. New York: Marshall Cavendish Benchmark, 2009.

Gordon, Sherri Mabry. *The Evolution Debate: Darwinism vs. Intelligent Design*. Berkeley Heights, NJ: Enslow Publishers, 2009.

Johnson, Rebecca L. *Genetics*. Minneapolis: Lerner Publishing Group, 2006.

Jusdon, Karen. *Religion and Government: Should They Mix?* New York: Marshall Cavendish Benchmark, 2010.

King, David C. *Charles Darwin*. New York: DK, 2006.

Whiting, Jim. *The Scopes Monkey Trial*. Hockessin, DE: Mitchell Lane Publishers, 2007.

DVDs

Evolution, WGBH Boston Video, 2001.

Inherit the Wind, MGM/UA Home Video, 2001.

Intelligent Design vs. Evolution, Films for the Humanities and Sciences, 2006.

The Scopes Trial Inherit the Truth: The Story as You've Never Seen It, Bryan College, 2007.

Websites

Darwin

www.amnh.org/exhibitions/darwin

This site provides an introduction to Darwin's life and theories, based on an exhibit at the American Museum of Natural History. Film and audio clips from scientists add personal views to the presentation.

The Discovery Institute

www.discovery.org

The Discovery Institute presents the works of scholars from many fields at its website, including scientists who promote intelligent design. The site also has videos of members' presentations as well as their blogs.

Evolution

www.pbs.org/wgbh/evolution

Based on the four-part series shown on PBS, this website gives an in-depth look at the history of evolutionary science. The Evolution Library section provides links to hundreds of sites on such topics as the evidence for evolution; human evolution; science, faith, and politics; and the nature of scientific study itself.

The Evolution Controversy
www.law.umkc.edu/faculty/projects/ftrials/conlaw/evolution.
htm
Law professor Doug Linder explores the legal battles over
evolution in the United States, starting with the *Scopes* trial
and continuing through *Kitzmiller v. Dover*. He includes links
to both pro- and anti-evolution websites.

Institute for Creation Research
www.icr.org
The site for the organization founded by Henry M. Morris
in 1970 offers information on creation science for parents,
students, teachers, and ministers. Articles from the IRC's
magazine, *Acts & Facts*, provide the latest arguments for
creation science and against Darwinian evolution.

Bibliography

Books

Allen, Leslie H., ed. *Bryan and Darrow at Dayton: The Record and Documents of the "Bible Evolution Trial."* New York: Arthur Lee, 1925.

The Annals of America, vol. 10. Chicago: Encyclopedia Britannica, 1968.

Behe, Michael J. *Darwin's Black Box: The Biochemical Challenge to Evolution*. New York: Touchstone, 1996.

Bowler, Peter J. *Monkey Trials and Gorilla Sermons: Evolution and Christianity from Darwin to Intelligent Design*. Cambridge: Harvard University Press, 2007.

Browne, Janet. *Charles Darwin: The Power of Place*. Princeton, NJ: Princeton University Press, 2002.

Cherny, Robert A. *A Righteous Cause: The Life of William Jennings Bryan*. Boston: Little, Brown and Company, 1985.

Cottrell, Robert C. *Roger Nash Baldwin and the American Civil Liberties Union*. New York: Columbia University Press, 2000.

Darrow, Clarence. *The Story of My Life*. Reprint. New York: Da Capo Press, 1996.

Darwin, Charles. *The Autobiography of Charles Darwin, 1809–1882*. Edited by Nora Barlow. New York: W. W. Norton & Company, 1958; reissue 2005.

Dembski, William A. *The Design Revolution: Answering the Toughest Questions About Intelligent Design*. Downers Grove, IL: InterVarsity Press.

Hofstadter, Richard. *Anti-Intellectualism in American Life*. New York: Vintage Books, 1963.

————. *Social Darwinism in American Thought*, rev. ed. Boston: Beacon Press, 1955.

Hood, Ralph W., et al. *The Psychology of Religious Fundamentalism*. New York: Guilford Press, 2005.

Israel, Charles A. *Before Scopes: Evangelical Education and Evolution in Tennessee, 1870–1925*. Athens: The University of Georgia Press, 2004.

Jensen, Richard J. *Clarence Darrow: The Creation of an American Myth*. New York: Greenwood Press, 1992.

Johnson, Philip E. *Darwin on Trial*. Washington, DC: Regnery Gateway, 1991.

Kazin, Michael. *A Godly Hero: The Life of William Jennings Bryan*. New York: Anchor Books, 2006.

Larson, Edward J. *Summer for the Gods*. New York: Basic Books, 1997.

Levine, Lawrence W. *Defender of the Faith: William Jennings Bryan: The Last Decade, 1915–1925*. New York: Oxford University Press, 1965.

Lienesch, Michael. *In the Beginning: Fundamentalism, the Scopes Trial, and the Making of the Antievolution Movement*. Chapel Hill: University of North Carolina Press, 2007.

Livingstone, David N. *Darwin's Forgotten Defenders: The Encounter Between Evangelical Theology and Evolutionary Thought*. Grand Rapids, MI: William B. Eerdmans Publishing Company, 1987.

Lynch, John M. *Darwin's Theory of Natural Selection: British Responses, 1859–1871*. Bristol, England: Thoemmes Press, 2001.

Marsden, George M. *Fundamentalism and American Culture*. 2nd ed. New York: Oxford Press, 2006.

Mencken, H. L. *The Vintage Mencken*. Gathered by Alistair Cooke. New York: Vintage Books, 1955.

Numbers, Ronald L. *The Creationists*. New York: Alfred A. Knopf, 1992.

Rodgers, Marion Elizabeth. *Mencken: The American Iconoclast*. New York: Oxford University Press, 2005.

Scott, Eugenie. *Evolution vs. Creationism: An Introduction*. Berkeley: University of California Press, 2004, p. 100.

Wills, Garry. *Under God: Religion in American Politics*. New York: Simon and Schuster, 1990.

Winthrop, John. *The Journal of John Winthrop, 1630–1649*. Abridged edition. Edited by Richard S. Dunn and Laetitia Yeandle. Cambridge: The Belknap Press of Harvard University, 1996.

Websites and Books Online

Babbage, Charles. *The Bridgewater Treatises on the Power Wisdom and Goodness of God as Manifested in the Creation*. Available online at the Victorian Web, www.victorianweb.org/science/bridgewater.html.

———. *The Ninth Bridgewater Treatise*. London: John Murray, 1838, pp. iv, xv. Available online at www.archive.org/stream/ninthbridgewate01babbgoog.

Bryan, William Jennings. *In His Image*. Electronic version at Project Gutenberg, www.gutenberg.org/files/12744/12744-8.txt.

———. *The Menace of Darwinism*. New York: Fleming H. Revell Company, 1922. Available online at http://ia341013.us.archive.org/3/items/menaceofdarwinis00brya/menaceofdarwinis00brya.pdf.

The Darwin Correspondence Project, www.darwinproject.ac.uk/darwinletters/calendar/entry-2548.html.

Famous Trials in American History: The Scopes Trial, www.law.umkc.edu/faculty/projects/ftrials/scopes/tennstat.htm.

Galileo's Battle for the Heavens, www.pbs.org/wgbh/nova/galileo/science.html.

Hodge, Charles. *What Is Darwinism?* Princeton, NJ: Scribner, Armstrong & Company, 1874. Available online at Project Gutenberg, www.gutenberg.org/files/19192/19192-h/19192-h.htm.

Hunter, George William. *A Civic Biology Presented in Problems.* New York: American Book Company, 1914. Available online at http://books.google.com/books?id=C8EXAAAAIAAJ&dq=george+william+hunter+civic+biology&printsec=frontcover&source=bl&ots=qQsD6k6mbC&sig=LmNVXogemKHVhb62gEFCWdHLbdM&hl=en&ei=rpBTSu_aGZOEtweZ6JSbCA&sa=X&oi=book_result&ct=result&resnum=1.

The John Ray Initiative, www.jri.org.uk/ray/cal/design.htm.

Monkey Trial. *American Experience,* www.pbs.org/wgbh/amex/monkeytrial/filmmore/pt.html.

Understanding Evolution, http://evolution.berkeley.edu/evo library/home.php.

Whewell, William. *Astronomy and General Physics Considered with Reference to Natural Theology*. London: William Pickering, 1836. Available online at http://books.google.com/books?id= iRwAAAAAQAAJ&pg=PA333&dq=Astronomy+and+Gen eral+Physics+Considered+with+Reference+to+Natural+The ology&output=text#c_top.

Plus websites listed in Further Information.

Web and Newspaper Articles

"As Expected, Bryan Wins." *Chicago Tribune*, 22 July 1925, p. 8.

"Attacks W.J.B.: Preacher Says Bryan's Article on Revolution Works Injury to Bible." *New York Times*, 12 March 1922, p. 91.

"Big Crowd Watches Trial Under Trees." *New York Times*, 21 July 1925, p. 1.

"Broadcast of Scopes Trial Unprecedented." *Chicago Tribune*, 5 July 1925, p. C6.

"Can Science and Religion Co-exist in Harmony?" Pew Research Center Publications, 22 June 2009. Available online at http://pewresearch.org/pubs/1259/can-science-and-faith-be-reconciled.

Collopy, Peter Sachs. "George Frederick Wright and the Harmony of Science and Revelation." Honors Thesis,

Oberlin College, 2007. Available online at http://collopy.net/projects/2007/Wright.pdf.

"Decision Today Is Likely; Judge Will Also Decide on Whether He Will Hear Scientists." *New York Times*, 14 July 1925, p. 1.

Edwards v. Aguillard. Available online at http://supreme.justia.com/us/482/578/case.html.

Epperson v. Arkansas. Available online at http://supreme.justia.com/us/393/97/case.html.

"Evolution and Creationism in Schools." The National Academies, www.nationalacademies.org/evolution/InSchools.html.

Heuman, Linda. "The Evolution of Ken Miller." *Brown Alumni Magazine*, November/December 2005, pp. 28–37. Available online at www.heumanwrites.com/stories/Brown_Alumni_Magazine__Evolution_of_Ken_Miller.pdf.

Irvine, Chris. "Vatican Claims Darwin's Theory of Evolution Is Compatible with Christianity. *Daily Telegraph*, 11 February 2009. Available online at www.telegraph.co.uk/news/newstopics/religion/4588289/The-Vatican-claims-Darwins-theory-of-evolution-is-compatible-with-Christianity.html.

Kinsley, Philip. "Scopes Case a 'Duel to the Death': W.J.B." *Chicago Tribune*, 8 July 1925, p. 1.

Kitzmiller v. Dover. Available online at The TalkOrigins Archive, www.talkorigins.org/faqs/dover/kitzmiller_v_dover_decision.html.

Mencken, H. L. "Fundamentalism: Divine and Secular." *Chicago Tribune*, 20 September 1925, p. E1.

————. "Malone the Victor, Even Though Court Sides with Opponents, Says Mencken," *Baltimore Evening Sun*, 17 July 1925. Available online at Positive Atheism, www.positiveatheism.org/hist/menck04.htm#SCOPES9.

Meyer, Stephen C. "Intelligent Design Is Not Creationism." *Daily Telegraph*, 28 January 2006. Available online at www.telegraph.co.uk/comment/personal-view/3622692/Intelligent-design-is-not-creationism.html.

Nelson, Valerie J. "Henry Morris, 87; 1961 Book Is Credited With Reviving the Creationism Movement." *Los Angeles Times*, 3 March 2006. Available online at http://articles.latimes.com/2006/mar/03/local/me-morris3?pg=1.

Rodgers, Ann. "Vatican Conference a Sign Church, Evolution Co-exist." *Pittsburgh Post-Gazette*, 1 March 2009. Available online at www.post-gazette.com/pg/09060/952458-51.stm.

Whitcomb, John C. "The Intelligent Design Movement." Answers in Genesis.org, 21 September 2005. Available online at www.answersingenesis.org/docs2005/0921whitcomb_pt 2.asp.

Index

Page numbers in **boldface** are illustrations.

About the Author

A history graduate of the University of Connecticut, free-lance author Michael Burgan has written more than 150 fiction and nonfiction books for children, as well as articles for adults. He has written several books on World War II, the cold war, and U.S foreign policy. Burgan is a recipient of an Educational Press Association of America award.